D0253209

GET SATISFIED

Get
SATISFIED

HOW

TWENTY PEOPLE

LIKE *You* FOUND

THE SATISFACTION

OF ENOUGH

Foreword by PETER C. WHYBROW, M.D.

Edited by CAROL HOLST

ISBN-10: 0974380687

ISBN-13: 978-0974380681

Books are available at special discounts when purchased in bulk for
premiums and sales promotions, as well as for fund-raising or educational uses.
Special editions or book excerpts can be created to customer specifications.
For details and further information, contact:

Special Sales Director
Easton Studio Press
P.O. Box 3131
Westport, CT 06880
(203) 454-4454
www.eastonsp.com

www.postconsumers.com

Postconsumers
P.O. Box 9955
Glendale, CA 91226
USA

Printed in Canada

SECOND PRINTING: DECEMBER 2009

10 9 8 7 6 5 4 3 2

Cover and interior book design by Barbara M. Bachman

*Bob Marley quoted lyrics on page v from the song "Exodus,"
on the album "Exodus," Polygram Records, 1977*

"Open your eyes, look within.

Are you satisfied with the life you're livin'?"

—BOB MARLEY

CONTENTS

PERSONAL STORIES OF SATISFACTION

Resolving Dramatic Challenges   1

Discovering the Sanity Within   35

FOREWORD

•

$\mathcal{S}$TORYTELLING IS AN ANCIENT ART.

Storytelling reflects the patterning of the human mind—the ordering of a random stockpile of personal experience into a meaningful, coherent, and unfolding theme. For each of us, in our journey along life's pebbled path, it is story that binds the start to the finish. And when stories are shared they can entertain, explain, and teach.

So I was reminded, on a recent visit to London, when I found myself standing in front of William Hogarth's *A Rake's Progress* at the Tate Gallery. Hogarth's story of Tom Moneypenny Rakewell is familiar: a young man of good education, finding himself in sudden wealth at the death of his miserly father, turns to spendthrift ways in ardent imitation of the profligate life of the aristocrat.

In the course of eight detailed and engaging tableaus the young Oxford graduate, seduced by luxury fever and exploited by the greed of others, is seen to drift from opulence and material abundance to the debtor's prison, ultimately to end his days in the madhouse. Tom, as Hogarth makes clear, is destroyed in his person by what today we might call a nasty case of addictive consumption. In short Tom loses control of his life's story, as is portrayed in these words of a contemporary writer: "Losing a thousand pounds . . . in a night Tom bets insanely on his horses at Epsom or Newmarket only to lose—lose—lose; but he is in the charmed circle; the mania is working—nothing can hold him back."

William Hogarth, standing a little under five feet in his socks, irreverent, pugnacious, and a snappy dresser, was an inveterate storyteller and a much-loved critic of the political and cultural issues of his time. In fact Hogarth lived in a period of rapid social change not dissimilar to our own. The series of paintings *A Harlot's Progress* and *A Rake's Progress,* and the engraved prints from those works that made him famous (and rich), were a runaway success in the 1730s, the era of market speculation and emerging global trade most remembered now for the scandal of the South Sea Bubble. The rapid growth of commerce and the pressures of a burgeoning market economy, the rapidly increasing urban population, and a growing freedom of individual expression together with its associated disruption of the familiar social order was, for many, a source of both wonder and anxiety. The turmoil fostered a demand for guidelines and for models of behavior that the writers and artists of the day, in books and magazines—and Hogarth in his social portraiture of cautionary tales—sought to satisfy.

If this all sounds strangely familiar—with today's self-help books, reality TV shows, and good-life gurus promising the "secret" to self-discovery and riches—it is because in America an addictive mania is once again the contemporary experience. But today there are some important twists. First, never in the history of our species have we experienced such abundance—of material goods, of information, and of choice—as we do now in America and in the developed world. Secondly, no longer are the persons caught up in the acquisitive frenzy numbered in their thousands, as in Hogarth's time, but rather in their millions. The craving and blind social striving for "stuff" and more "stuff" that drove Tom Rakewell to his ruin is now fostered as America's preferred route to happiness by a daily blizzard of mind-numbing promotion. In consequence, for many in our society the drive for profit has become a way of life where more will never be enough.

In American culture we increasingly worship the market as an ideology rather than recognizing it for what it is—a natural product of human social evolution and a set of valuable tools through which we may shape a healthful and equitable society. Across the globe technology has dramatically changed the checks and balances that regulate the marketplace. America's traditional immigrant values of resourcefulness, thrift, prudence, and an abiding concern for family and community have been hijacked by a commercially driven, all-consuming self-interest that is rapidly making us sick, both as individuals and as a society.

Our species has a long lineage, but in that evolution the social intelligence and mindful planning that makes us human arrived only recently, almost as an afterthought. By instinct we are geared for individual survival—curious, reward driven and self-absorbed. These instinctual strivings are the engines of the market, as was first described by the patron saint of American capitalism, Adam Smith (who was a teenager when Hogarth first came to wide public attention). But in Smith's original vision, published in 1776 in *An Inquiry into the Wealth of Nations*, the tethers of community and concern for the well-being of others were essential to the smooth operation of the "invisible hand"—Smith's metaphor for the dynamic social forces that guide a self-regulating market society.

But what Smith failed to recognize in his social model, writing before the industrial revolution, was that human beings are poorly equipped to cope with extraordinary material abundance, as is evident from the U.S. experience. Sadly, in our demand-driven, information-saturated, turbo-charged world that never sleeps—where the nurturing, constraining infrastructure of vibrant community is increasingly neglected and eroding—Adam Smith's invisible hand is fast losing its grip.

Seduced by the enticements of a global market, the American consumer has in recent decades fallen victim to an orgy of consumption that is a worthy successor to the cautionary tale of Tom Rakewell himself. Thus while America's productivity per person-hour is comparable to that of most European nations, our material consumption per person is now greater by one-third. And there are consequences to our profligate spending, including a runaway personal and national debt, overwork, sleep deprivation, anxiety, a growing income gap between the rich and the poor, and a declining social mobility—to name but a few. Indeed, the evidence is growing that unless we Americans can find intelligent self-constraint, we will soon run ourselves into the ground, depleting not only vital physical resources but also eroding the economic strength, the personal health, and that social capital that is essential to sustaining a vibrant culture.

Fortunately, as this reality begins to hit home, the tide is turning against such blind consumption. In Britain an interesting, indeed radical, group of young people of which William Hogarth would have been proud—known provocatively as the New Puritans—are championing a personal code of conduct that eschews profligate spending in favor of a lifestyle that emphasizes health, freedom from personal debt, and social interdependence. Similarly, a growing number of Americans—of which the twenty stories in this volume are representative—are recognizing that personal wisdom can grow only from an honest reckoning of self-need and how technology and the market can best serve those needs.

I believe that the publication of this book by Postconsumers is vital evidence that the tide of sentiment is now turning in America, as in Europe—that there is an awakening to the knowledge that a satisfying personal narrative must unfold with an awareness of each precious moment and a true appreciation of others. A series of natural disasters and the skyrocketing price of oil may have helped focus this awakening that it is not technology itself that will deliver personal happiness, or achieve social progress, but rather its wise and intelligent application. If a free market society—an ownership society—is to work then part of that ownership must be held in collective responsibility, as an investment in the "common wealth" that nurtures each of us. In these troubled times it is important to remember that human beings became dominant on this planet not because of our individual intelligence, but because of our collective social savvy that harnessed that intelligence.

Personal identity and self-fulfillment emerge through individual experience in communion with others. It has always been so. It was true in Hogarth's time, as his social portraits still proclaim, and it is equally true today. It is pleasure—often all too fleeting—that is to be found in material acquisition. Such pleasures should be savored, but happiness and contentment in life are something else. Rarely are they to be found in material pursuit, as *A Rake's Progress* reminds us. Rather, happiness and contentment have a way of welling up unexpectedly, as you will discover in the following stories—compelling stories of honest self-reflection that will entertain, explain, and teach. Enjoy the ancient art!

And tell your own story. Others will be listening.

—*Peter C. Whybrow, M.D.*

DIRECTOR, Semel Institute for
Neuroscience and Human Behavior, UCLA
AUTHOR, *American Mania: When More is Not Enough*
Los Angeles, May 2007

INTRODUCTION AND
ACKNOWLEDGMENTS

•

I don't have enough. Not nearly enough. Not only that, I'm not satisfied. I just can't manage to get a good hold on one without the other, since satisfaction and enough are two well-matched sides of the same coin.

Oh, I have enough coin, although our society tells me that it's generally impossible to have enough money. And I have enough clothes, enough shoes, enough light fixtures, and enough refrigerator magnets, although magazines try to convince me otherwise. I'm really very satisfied with the stuff in my life, the focus of my activities, and the people with whom I share it all.

But I simply don't have enough breaths, enough yelps, enough shrieks, enough eardrum-splitting ways to process the beauty that is life on this planet. Basically, I don't have enough life itself—can't seem to soak it up and give back nearly enough. Just can't get satisfied. So far.

As it turns out, the immense majority of people in this country are in a similar boat, one way or another. Here are hundreds of millions of people who have more than most in the world and yet experience continual gnawing, yearning, gamut-stretching craving to the depths of their beings. It might be said that satisfaction is the one thing Americans need most that most eludes them.

Figuring that there must be at least a few people out there who have found *the satisfaction of enough* in our culture and who would like to share their stories, we put out a national call for submissions to this book. Amazingly, we were flattened straightaway by the avalanche.

A bowled-over editorial committee grinned and selected the following eleven women and nine men from across the country with ages ranging in the twenties, thirties, forties, fifties, sixties, and seventies. All are superb writers and all have compelling stories from the perspective of the general public (rather than the self-selected few "living under rocks in Topanga" as our advocate Ed Begley Jr. jokes). Whether they've chosen to be satisfied with a little or a lot, they are all wealthy in their contentment.

In fact, they represent the broadest possible continuum of Americans from our deluge who have sought and found simpler, more satisfying lives. We believe this book is just the beginning of America's new love affair with *the satisfaction of enough.*

This brings up an important perspective to emphasize about joyfully dropping needless wanting in a desperate world filled with extreme wanting, and in a confused country obsessed with wanting for the sake of wanting: everyone's ideas about wanting are different. These twenty authentic stories cover a spectrum of those underlying ideas and a range of self-styled, personal solutions—no one size fits all. It's ultimately up to me to decide where my peace of mind lies, as each of you may decide yours.

And now a few words about who we are. Easton Studio Press is publishing this book for us, Postconsumers, an educational company helping to move our society beyond addictive consumerism. We advocate mindful consumption based on each person's core values, rather than an endless quest for "stuff." There's just nothing like celebrating the centrality of community, family, nature, and meaning in our lives. It casts a whole new light on current economic upheavals, to say the least.

One of the principal offerings at our website www.postconsumers.com is the companion "how to" interactive module for this book, *"Get Satisfied: How to Find the Satisfaction of Enough."* Michael Beck is the primary author, with significant contributions by Yukio Okano, Ph.D., a clinical psychologist at Kaiser Permanente. It's framed on a pioneering book—*American Mania: When More Is Not Enough*—by the director of the Semel Institute for Neuroscience and Human Behavior at UCLA, Peter C. Whybrow, M.D. That book informs much of the mental health background for our work, which is produced in cooperation with the Semel Institute.

Postconsumers also offers a rare treat these days: all the humor you can wish for. Our website's expanding Get Satisfied Cartoon Gallery is a gift to the consumer world from Hollywood animator Mike Swofford. He lent his skills to the highly successful *Simpsons Movie* and played a seminal role in such Disney classics as *The Little Mermaid, Beauty and the Beast, Aladdin,* and *The Lion King.*

As an educational company, Postconsumers is grounded in professional market research recently conducted by The Pollux Group, Inc. When asked about their own consumption behavior, most respondents felt that they themselves did not have a problem, but that many of their friends and acquaintances—and even significant others—did. David Atkins, president of The Pollux Group, Inc., headed the design team for our "Exploratory Research on Materialism" study, which reached people where they are rather than simply where we are. Fred Adler, Ph.D. and Michael Beck also made valuable contributions to the research team.

Gratitude for help with this book goes first and foremost to the ingenious authors who reveal the founts of their successes in the following chapters, and to all those who submitted their exceptional writing. Theirs is the stuff of a satisfied America, a miracle in the making. And none of us would be half as effective in countering American mania without Peter C. Whybrow, M.D., and his masterful foreword to this book. It is the deep backdrop for our endeavors and shows that self-interest, the bedrock of these chapters, is self-constraint.

Among the fabulous activists in this field, Wanda Urbanska and Cecile Andrews are especially inspirational and helpful to our efforts. The *Simple Living with Wanda Urbanska* national public television series is a lifelong anchor, and the books they have written are transformational.

Thanks also go to Jill Aylard, Michael Beck, Maria Hodkins, and Stan King of the editorial committee, as well as to advisors Randy Gold and Thurman Couch. Barbara Bachman is our extraordinary book designer. Booktrix, Easton Studio Press, and Ripe Media stars David Wilk, Heather Richman, and Chris Simental continually help everything unfold like clockwork, the experts behind the scenes who deserve special applause.

Speaking of stars, Ed Begley Jr. and Alexandra Paul have freely given us their stunning Hollywood voices for many years. They are not only bestowing *Get Satisfied* with celebrity power, but also look really, really good doing it. The postconsumers trend is sexy! Our friends at the Simple Living Network in cyberspace are cool too, and get all the thanks for the comprehensive bibliography.

Let's face it: we're all really sexy in this field. The folks in the Take Back Your Time field are pretty darn sexy too.

That leaves you, dear readers, who will find at least one revelation in these pages, guaranteed. The *satisfaction of enough* has a thousand facets here and a million to come as the movement grows with your added voices. Rest assured that this guarantee comes from someone who, every moment, knows the massive craving for more.

Let's *get satisfied* together.

—*Carol Holst*

ORGANIZING THIS
EXPLORATION

•

by Michael Beck

H OW CAN YOU BEGIN TO EXPLORE WHETHER YOU HAVE enough to be richly satisfied or, as some would venture, to be happy with life?

Our popular culture and media hold forth definite answers: get wealthy, win the lottery, or work (exceedingly) hard and make it big. These messages can get boring in their repetitiveness.

Our twenty authors, on the other hand, offer twenty very different answers, each one fascinating because each is unique. The one thing they have in common is that all these writers have looked within and found a personal formula for how to be satisfied with their lives—in other words, for how to say, "This is plenty."

On considering these stories, in fact, we have been struck by the great diversity of perspectives and solutions that they represent. Nonetheless, we have found that these accounts fall loosely into five categories. Of course, we invite each reader to group them (or ungroup them) as they see fit. But here we have organized the chapters under these broad types of experiences:

Resolving Dramatic Challenges
Discovering the Sanity Within

"Unstuffing" One's Life
The Wonderment of Enough
Cruising to Satisfaction

PERSONAL STORIES

of

Satisfaction

Resolving Dramatic

Challenges

■

THE PHOENIX RISING

•

by J. Eva Nagel

$\mathcal{S}$OMETIMES CHANGE SNEAKS UP ON YOU. IT MIGHT COME like a sprite in the night urging you to pack your bags and move to Sedona. Sometimes change saunters in like an unemployed hustler in cowboy boots and has its way with you. Not being a particularly subtle woman, I got the version of change that hits you over the head with a frying pan and squawks, "Yoo-hoo, move your rear end."

There I was on the verge of the second half of my life, with only the youngest of my four children still at home—my expectations clear, my doctoral dissertation almost complete, my life settled into an abundant but comfortable routine. Then I got this wake-up call in the middle of the night, in the middle of autumn, in the middle of my fiftieth year. Some have been heard to say that the world will end in fire. I was presented with this scorching form of endings, little knowing it was a beginning in disguise. My house burned. Not down exactly . . . more like up.

One quiet Sunday evening I went to bed in our comfortable old house, completely engrossed in my ordinary, albeit frenzied life replete with shoulds, musts, and highly significant ought-tos. My appointment book rested on the nightstand, brimming with expectations. A few hours later, I was bedless, clothesless, homeless, and appointment free.

Have you ever thought about the fire possibility? I had. Here's how my imagined plan went for me: Okay, if there's a fire, first get the kids out, then the animals. If there is any time left, go for the photo albums. Now this plan sounds simple, right? The kid, once awakened, got out on his own; the animals needed no convincing—they were long gone. The cats were giving the house a wide berth, the dog was found shivering under our car. But this "save the photo albums" command . . . sounds simple, right? I'd always pictured tucking them under my arms and running out of the house. Well, I was soon forced to think again. I'd been raising four kids and various honorary stepkids for twenty-seven years. That's a lot of pictures! Sixteen photo albums don't fit easily under two arms.

I stood in the downstairs hallway, after calling 911, with one album tucked under each arm, fourteen to go. Go where? I moved toward the guest room away from the fire. Wait a minute. What if the whole house burns down? I know . . . I'll stack them out the back door. No. The fire hoses might soak them. I stood there swaying with indecision. Finally, I raced to the back door, dumped the recyclables out of their bin, carried the plastic container back to the house, loaded in the photo albums, and dragged the bin back out into the yard.

I'm doing great, but this is as far as my imagined scenario ever got—the children, the pets, the photo albums are safe—now what do I save? Volunteer firefighters were tromping around upstairs at this point and clambering onto our metal roof. In my big rubber boots and eerie calm, I went back into the burning house, to our untouched, still-normal, downstairs reading room.

I turn toward the shelves of books and it hits me: *I am going to lose all of you.* My life was on those shelves: books on childbirth, gardening, environmental issues; an entire shelf on Waldorf education, women's issues, and healing guides; Native American religion, a huge collection of fairy and folk tales, another of poetry. What about the biographies? And the novels! The ones I loved and read aloud to my sons and daughters: *The Lion, the Witch and the Wardrobe; The Indian in the Cupboard; A Story Like the Wind.* I took a deep breath and whispered, "You were terrific. I've loved you. Now I bid you goodbye." A feeling of floating free crept into me. All those books accumulate a great deal of dust.

"What are you doing in here?" bellowed the helmeted fireman, breaking through my Kerouac-like reverie and making it clear that I was no longer wanted or needed in my own home. I spent the next few hours on my front lawn, shivering, with plenty of time to think. I imagined setting forth into the rest of my life, free and unfettered, with nothing to tie me down and fray my soul. Before that night, I had so many clothes I couldn't decide what to wear in the morning. I had way too many electrical gadgets: toasters, juicers, waffle irons, boom boxes, and answering machines. These things weren't me. I could do without them.

If I were a bona fide flower child, as I was long ago, my story would end here and I'd be living in a yurt on the ashes of my house with a few charred pots and a warm sleeping bag, dispensing wisdom in short, easily digestible segments. The truth is a lot messier and considerably less picturesque. As the new day lightened the sky, the firefighters let us back into our home. It hadn't burned down; it had merely burned. It hadn't turned into purified ashes to blow away in the wind, but into a sodden, reeking mess. The alchemy failed. My lead didn't turn into gold, it merely melted into clumps. The tin roof of our house and the eastern walls were gone. My books were still there, now wet and smelly. My life wasn't liberated and simplified, but complicated and inconvenienced.

"We will live simply," my sometimes simple-minded husband said the next morning, over instant coffee. "We don't need much." Explain to me, I thought, how to live simply with three jobs, two offices, doctoral thesis deadlines, volunteer responsibilities, three rental units, a hungry teenager, two cats, a dog, and a turtle? Someone better break it to him gently: those carefree, Woodstock days are gone.

Did I mention my doctoral research? I was close to the final approach on my doctoral thesis. To this glorious end, I'd amassed a three-foot stack of photocopied research articles sorted by categories. Most of these survived the fire (Yay!), but not the fire hoses (Boo!). The man at the next booth in the sushi restaurant, overhearing my despair, told me to put them in the freezer. It would stop the rotting process and buy me some time.

Thank goodness for friends! I arrived at Jane's house that night, dragging two garbage bags filled with sticky, crumbling papers. They fit perfectly between the pop tarts and the turkey in her basement freezer. There they waited for weeks until I was settled in a rental unit with an oven. I then began peeling and baking my papers in small slices. Just as with pancakes, the skill is in the flipping: not too soon, or the dampness will cause mildew and not too late, since the smell of charred paper doesn't whet the appetite. If you open my office closet and inhale, you'll find my resurrected research.

Friends asked us how our fourteen-year-old son was doing. I didn't know. After the first confused weeks sleeping in a motel and at the homes of various friends, he seemed completely unaffected. He was busy with his own life and this did not seem to place that high on his Richter scale. Then one day, almost two months after the fire, he said longingly, "You know what I really miss?" *Oh boy, I thought, here it comes at last. He's buried this for so long. Am I ready to deal with his psychological scars?*

"No," I said, sitting down next to him and laying my hand gently upon his arm, "What is it, honey?"

"Tall glasses," he answered from the depths of his soul.

"Tall glasses?" I gulped in confusion.

"Yup. The glasses here are too small for a good drink."

The writer Annie Lamott says that courage is fear that has said its prayers. Maybe two dozen years of family songs and prayers, tears and laughter, joys and sorrows under those 250 year-old living room beams had counted for something, because we never felt afraid. This isn't the story of tragedy. Tragedy is babies suffering. Tragedy is mothers dying young. Tragedy is planes crashing and buildings crumbling. This fire wasn't a tragedy. I keep searching for a word that is stronger than inconvenience, but less than disaster. Instead I'm left with the words of a well-fed bear: "Oh, bother."

The fire was a wake-up call. Okay, I'm wide awake now. I'm paying attention. I see the friends who rallied with food, blankets, and all their extra attic furniture. I see our family unified and ready to celebrate. I see my husband who makes each drama into the latest new adventure. I see blessings everywhere I turn. I see how transformation creeps into the roofless house of my being and pushes me out to greet it.

Who am I? What do I want? What matters most in my life? It might have been the burning bush speaking to me from my living room, but these are the *little* questions that started tugging at my untied shoelaces. Even while I was knee-deep in cleanup, I could not ignore their insistent demand.

Did our life change post-inferno? Of course it did, but it doesn't look that much simpler. We still have four kids (plus one teenage niece), a menagerie of entitled pets, and those pesky jobs and other responsibilities. We didn't move into a yurt, convert our TV into an altar, or start biking to work. Our priorities, however, are as clear as a crisp autumn evening. Taken in any order, my family remains right up there at the top of the list. We celebrate everything possible: birthdays, religious holidays, various milestones, and unique sunny days. I take immeasurable satisfaction in watching my children evolve into impressive adults who are already making a difference in the world. It is like winning the lottery!

Then there is health. My husband became an

exuberant jock in middle age and I am scrambling to keep up. Challenging bike trips push me to a new sense of well-being. We relish good food locally grown, some of it harvested only a few feet away in our garden. My latest challenge is to rest when I am tired. What a concept! I am filling my life with welcoming spaces of deep breaths. Afternoon naps may be the cure for the world's problems. I am thinking of lobbying for a new law: mandatory naps for all.

Let's not forget joy. It has a way of filling those spaces when given a chance. It spreads like . . . could it be? . . . wildfire. And there is always my husband's mantra—"Are we having fun yet?"—to remind me. These priorities are challenged by the importance of giving back. There are so many ways to do it. Mentoring young people is as natural as breathing now. They keep me from atrophying into a crusty old fart. My husband, Lee, works in a free medical clinic near our office and goes on a medical mission to Guatemala; I have a project in partnership with a women's cooperative in Zimbabwe. Nothing like a trip to Africa to remind us of how much less we need. Giving back should be called getting back because I am the one who is blessed by it.

And, of course, there is gratitude. We don't wait for Thanksgiving to give thanks for our blessings—I go to sleep and wake up with a hallelujah. It isn't the books on my shelves or the latest appliance in my kitchen, or even those precious photo albums that really matter to me. It is the life I lead today and every day. Whether this is the last day of my life or the first day of the rest of my life, I want to make it a good one.

So watch out for me. I am rising from the ashes—dusty and a wee bit discombobulated, but ready to fly. Like the phoenix, I came through the fire. Next time I might ask for ice instead of fire, or perhaps a brick house, but until then, this fire will definitely suffice.

THE GLAMOROUS LIFE

•

by Todra Payne

WHEN I WAS IN MY TWENTIES AND WORKING A DREAD-
ful desk job at a law firm, I dreamed of a glamorous career that would put me in the company of models and
actors. I didn't know what I wanted to do exactly, so for a
time I flirted with several possible career moves—actor,
playwright, fashion designer—but nothing seemed to fit
well until I stumbled onto makeup artistry. Creating col-
orful art is something that has always been a source of
enjoyment for me, even as a child.

In my teens, I kept myself in designer jeans and
Michael Jackson albums by selling my hand-painted T-
shirts and jean jackets. It was the eighties when air-
brushed art was king among teens, but I deliberately set
out to make money by painting fabric the way I imagined
the masters painted canvas—slowly and meticulously.
My Japanese pagodas and water-lily-covered lakes were
a marked departure from the fat bubble letters and
bulging-eyed cartoon characters that other teen artists
were hawking. My work sold. Sometimes I had back-
logged orders that forced me to paint through the night.

When I was seventeen, my entrepreneurial endeavors
came to a screeching halt because my mother, someone
who puts far more emphasis on education than self-ex-

pression, found me asleep at the kitchen table at sunrise. I was still wearing my Catholic school uniform from the day before. I had a paintbrush in my hand. My unfinished homework was sitting nearby.

At twenty-eight, I determined that makeup artistry wasn't such a far stretch from painting jean jackets, so I closed my eyes and leapt. I quit my desk job.

In New York City, any skill that makes others thinner, prettier, or richer is worth its weight in gold. And when, in three years, my part-time makeup work was earning me twice my former administrative salary, it seemed I'd certainly struck gold. I had an agent who contacted clients, sent out my portfolio, and managed my accounting. Faxes arrived for me with instructions to show up for *Elle, Harper's Bazaar,* or *Glamour* fashion and beauty shoots. I worked with some of the industry's top celebrities and models. My work and my name were frequently splashed across the glossies, and sometimes on television. It was all very exciting and I'm glad I got to live it, but I didn't know how to handle the money or the "fame" wisely.

I was making good money, but I certainly didn't have the funds my celebrity clients had. Being in their company sometimes made me forget that I couldn't afford the same $6,000 chair or $1,200 pants they were buying. I became consumed with having the latest and trendiest in everything. If we shot a new Roberto Cavalli dress on Tuesday, I was combing Barney's on Thursday, asking if they had it in. For me, it wasn't about keeping up with the Joneses, but about *being* the Joneses.

I remember one afternoon I showed up at Leelee

Sobieski's hotel room to do her makeup for a television appearance. She looked at me and said, "You look amazing. Where did you get those pants?" It was such a rush when a young Hollywood actress asked me where *I* shopped. Year after year, I continued on my spending expeditions with little regard for saving or paying estimated taxes.

It's pretty obvious where all of this was leading.

Six years later, I was in so much debt that I couldn't fathom how I'd crawl out, even with my day rate, which sometimes hit $1,700.

And then September 11th happened. Although I did not lose a loved one in the attacks, the experience changed me. How could it not? I stood on the corner of Seventh Avenue and Twelfth Street with my neighbors, watching the towers burn. I'll never forget the huge cloud of black smoke that lifted into the air. And the sound of sirens as ambulances and fire trucks rushed through the city streets.

At that moment, I started to look at life differently. I wondered where I was headed and what it all meant. In the big scheme of things, who cares if I had the same pair of Manolos that Carrie wore on *Sex in the City?*

In the weeks that followed, I lost my insatiable appetite for stuff.

I questioned everything.

I cried with friends who lost family members in the towers.

In the aftermath of the tragedy, every industry in New York suffered. The beauty work, in particular, wasn't pouring in as it had in the past. New Yorkers were trying to regain their bearings. The city streets, normally bursting with sound and energy, were eerily quiet except for sobs and the occasional question from a bewildered person walking the streets with pictures of loved ones. "Have you seen this person? He's missing." Many New Yorkers chose to leave their beloved city because the pain was too much. My new husband and I also decided to move out of New York and start over.

Today, we are living in a tiny city in central Pennsylvania that is far less glitzy and sexy than the Big Apple, but we are satisfied with it. We're living more sensible, intentional lives. We've mapped out where we are versus where we want to be in the near future. Because of my crazy spending habits from the past, we still owe a huge sum in back taxes and some other consumer debt, but we're paying everything back, dollar by dollar. We've had to learn to live moderately, but it doesn't feel like we're deprived. Instead, we are empowered by the decisions we make.

As a result of our experiences, we've learned to ask ourselves questions that help us reach our goals: *"Do we need to buy this or are we trying to fill some desire with this purchase?" "Should we wait until we can pay cash or perhaps wait until it's on sale?" "Will we get a good amount of use from this, or is it a trend item?"*

My husband works a nine-to-five job with a modest income. I work as a freelance writer and CFO of our household. One of the first things I set in place in our new life was a budget. In the past, I never knew where my money went. It just seemed to fly out of my hands before my bills arrived in the mail, leaving me with nothing but bad credit. Now, our bills are paid automatically from our checking account. Every month we go online and watch our debt dwindle. It's a great feeling. I no longer impulse shop. I clip coupons. (My mother almost passed out when I told her!) We share one car. And I don't own a television; fewer advertisements never hurt anyone.

We don't live paupers' lives. We buy designer clothes (at outlets), eat at fine restaurants, and take short vacations to refresh. I couldn't stand a life that is too austere after having such a glamorous existence, but I choose my splurges wisely.

Our diligence has paid off. Our credit is good and we're closing on our first house shortly. The house is small, but beautiful. And, most important, it's affordable. Our mortgage is half the cost of the rent I paid for a one-bedroom apartment in Manhattan's West Village. For us, *this* is living.

TO WALK A FINE LINE

•

By Michael Beck

HE SHIFT IN ATTITUDE THAT SAVED MY HEALTH—
perhaps my life—began with a date.

Laura was a fellow teacher I'd long seen as a friend.
But this evening, while we traded quips at the expense of
school bureaucracy, I became acutely aware of her wit,
her perspective, and, yes, her attractiveness.

As we drove back to my place, she turned to me. "So
tell me, are you still happy with your house?"

"Definitely. Though without your feedback I might
not have persevered in buying it."

"Always glad to help. Is this your permanent house or
do you see yourself moving on?"

An opening? "I'm happy with it for now. But once I'm
in a committed relationship, it would be a joint decision."

She shot back, "I don't see you ever getting married."

"Laura, I used to be a confirmed bachelor, but you
should know I've gotten past that."

"That's not my point." She hesitated. "Why would
any woman want to marry a man in his fifties who has so
little to show for his age as you do?"

Taken aback, I countered, "I feel comfortable with
what I have."

"Are you comfortable with that pathetic little stereo of yours that needs to be junked?"

Oh that. "It's old, but why should I replace it if it satisfies my needs?"

"Most men in their fifties would be satisfied with nothing less than a state-of-the-art home entertainment center."

With that, the conversation lapsed. When we reached my house, I neglected to invite her in—not that she seemed to notice.

This episode preyed on my mind for weeks. Of course it was a blow to my self-esteem to have a friend—supposedly a friend—flatly find me substandard. But I could resolve that. If I didn't make her cut on home entertainment centers, she certainly didn't make mine on friendship or values. Still, I felt inadequate. So I went over and looked—partly it *was* this years-old stereo from Sears clearance. Why didn't I just go out and buy something nice? I could afford it.

There were two problems with that.

First, I didn't want to hassle selecting just the right system, lugging it home, and hooking everything up, when my old one played music just fine.

Second, if I did so, it would just shift the onus to something else, like my car. Yes, I'd bought the Accord new, but that was 150,000 miles ago, and colleagues had begun to notice. Yet it drove just fine, and a new one *would* stress my budget.

Still, Laura had hit a nerve. Though I had never been acquisitive, I had always wanted to make a better show in that department. The issue wasn't Laura at all but my wanting to live by standards that I didn't particularly believe in. Understanding this lifted my spirits; with time I could remedy it.

I called Laura. Yes, she suspected she'd been a bit harsh. Was there anything in particular? I told her.

"That does sound judgmental," she acknowledged. I waited to see if she had anything to add. "I should probably watch that sort of thing more carefully."

It was close enough to an apology. I resolved not to point out that she'd actually done me a favor.

The incident faded, but several months later it resurfaced when I took a quiet, pleasant lady to dinner. As we were ferreting out common interests, she brightened, going for a surefire icebreaker: "Michael, what's your favorite TV program?"

I admitted that I didn't have any.

She frowned. "But there must be one thing you watch more than any other."

"Not in my case. You see, I don't own a TV."

She was dumbstruck—as in rendered speechless. I cautiously broke the silence. "Sherry, are you okay?"

"I've never known anyone . . . without a TV. I guess I don't know how to handle this." But gradually she managed, which led to an agreeable if not exactly sizzling evening.

As I drove home, I sensed a growing transformation; I wasn't TV-deprived, simply TV-free. My relaxation was reading, for which there was never enough time. What would befall those beckoning nature magazines, sci-fi novels, and Roman histories if I allowed a TV in?

I refocused on Sherry—and found myself hoping that,

for her sake, she could find a guy as crazy about TV as she was.

As for me, although I didn't pine for a fancy home entertainment center, neither did I aspire to be a church mouse. If my Accord started misbehaving, I would happily replace it. Meanwhile, the less spent on stuff for show, the more I'd have for things that counted, like saving for earlier retirement and travel—especially travel.

The latter is what made my teaching job ideal. Though I griped about the paperwork, the school calendar was a godsend. Our year-round schedule had two rotating short vacations rather than a single long one; my particular times in early spring and fall excelled for off-season trips. By my own lights, I had more than enough to be content, and with a growing confidence in my choices, my social life improved.

Now, it would have been nice if my job had cooperated. But, alas, a new weight of bureaucracy was settling upon classroom teachers. As a bilingual teacher, I loved instructing in both Spanish and English, but new rules shut the children out of English reading to focus on Spanish literacy. Though my colleagues and I knew the old way worked better, the district cited irrefutable studies (from a different country and sociological setting), so I was now toeing the line for standards I didn't accept. However, I was being paid to teach their standards, not mine, so I did my best to apply them in the classroom.

Despite my efforts, doing things the district's way was getting harder. At nearly every staff meeting they'd back up the truck to offload reams of paperwork larded with "rubrics" and other jargon as dense as legalese—but far less helpful. To cope, and to keep my blood pressure down, I focused on my improved social life, my next trip to some beautiful national park, and the everyday rewards of working with my fourth graders.

Then came a show stopper. Some oversized truck pulled up to disgorge that year's standardized tests. We sat there, scanning the high piles, while a week of creativity dissolved into testing, testing. Next they rolled in a surprise for the select among us, the bilingual teachers. More boxes thumped on the table: a second week of testing for Spanish readers only, the students most in need of more teaching. Batteries of testing—all in English.

My neighbor ventured, "Dorothy, why are we testing them in English when they only read Spanish?"

The coordinator was curt, "It's a state requirement."

I raised my hand. "Then why did they make us limit their reading to Spanish?"

"Because that's a district mandate."

Gosh, that certainly had to make everything okay. Dorothy admitted the kids would quickly mark at random, but we would still allot an entire week to ensure they got the exact answers to questions they couldn't read.

My hand was up again, genetic misprogramming maybe, unless the devil made me do it. "Do I understand we're being *ordered* to test our kids for a week, in the English we were forbidden to teach?"

"Mr. Beck." She scowled. "If you insist upon phrasing it that way, I cannot stop you. . . . Yes, Lizette, hopefully you have a reasonable question?"

I hadn't been fair; she was simply being paid to do it their way, as were all of us. Nonetheless, making up a week's lost teaching was typical of our growing workload. As it took its toll, I felt a familiar sense of inadequacy. By not keeping up with their labyrinth of mandates, I was falling short of the accountability the district kept promising was the last word in helping kids.

The fact that I utterly failed to share their enthusiasm recalled my encounter with Laura. But here I could not simply opt to teach as I knew best, nor could I quit outright this close to retirement. Remaining true to myself within this brave new system would prove far more challenging than dating. I did my best by focusing on my kids and their enthusiasm, antics, and crises.

The next school year greeted us with an exciting new learning matrix, i.e., an innovative assault on common sense. Years of reading programs grounded in experiential creativity morphed overnight into a lockstep skills-based model. Dutifully, I realigned to laser precision in skills, all in Spanish, to be tested later in English. But the new accountability proved far more exhausting.

Relentlessly, stress crept up. It began following me home, slipping into my sleep—deadlines, rubrics, documentation trails—tingeing my morning commute with resentment that made me snap at colleagues, and worse, at my kids.

Ominously, I started putting on weight.

Reluctantly, I kept my next doctor's appointment. After walking in as a patient he'd been monitoring, I walked out officially diabetic and hypertensive, clutching prescriptions, feeling punched in the stomach—my entirely too ample stomach. My ears rang with Dr. Wesley's lecture about it.

Time to see my counselor. Having already cut back on social life, now I needed to find yet more time to fix my health. At the end of the hour, Bernie summarized, "Michael, you can have your job. You can have your health. You can have a social life. In fact, you may pick any two of them."

It sank in. "This is pretty sobering."

"I am acquainted with the school district." His voice tightened. "My wife works for it."

That Sunday I hiked into my favorite canyon, pulled up a rock, peered at sycamore leaves fluttering against the sky, and opened my mind to major reassessment.

Five more years. I'd long planned to retire at sixty-two by putting away enough so I could live comfortably on pension and savings. I'd even dreamed of luxuries like an epic trip to New Zealand. . . . Except that now boarding a plane was doubtful—first they'd have to let me out of that nice, white, padded room.

The rustling leaves slowly soothed me into redefining "comfortable." By cutting back and saving more, I could retire in three years at sixty. This would require challenging adjustments to my lifestyle, such as the Accord, now acting up at 180,000 miles. No matter, I would drive it to the end.

More problematically, I needed to reconcile my vision of job performance with that of the bureaucracy. This simply had to be resolved, or I wouldn't even last three years. Within weeks, I worked out a method. First, get serious about taking paperwork craziness less to heart. Second, (breathe deeply here) cut back even more on travel and socializing to save both time and money. This tightrope walk offered satisfaction; it would sustain me until I was sixty.

Then I met Marianne.

We promptly fell for each other, and I was certain I'd finally found a partner that I could love and who shared my passions and values. There was one little hitch: my stress and time crunch—hard on her, though possibly harder on me. Bernie's admonition rang all too true.

Still, my new resolve and Marianne's support buoyed me through the first months of the next school year. A hope glimmered of work easing up. Then one Tuesday afternoon our principal convulsed the faculty meeting: as of immediately, all kids would read English only. California had just revoked bilingual education.

Understandably, there were questions. Wasn't there a six-month transition? Sure there was, but our school would just cut to the chase. What about books in English? Basal readers were being ordered; in the meantime, he was confident, we would be creative.

"Creative" led me to a half set of obsolete lower-grade readers in a dusty closet. What the heck, they were in English, and my kids could share when pages weren't missing. In any case, another situation quickly loomed: an enormous ratcheting up of pupil progress tracking.

The struggle to reconcile my ideal of teaching with the district's had just taken a new plunge. Soon, a classroom incident brought this vividly home. I caught two boys in the act of blending math with pocket video-game practice. Their outrageous excuses made me burst out laughing, with the whole class joining in. That didn't rescue the boys, but it sure helped the lesson, lightened the day for all of us, and eventually benefited the two culprits.

That evening, as I savored the memory, waves of nostalgia swept across me. Whatever had become of my career, the only meaningful one I'd ever known, once so ideal that I would almost regret going on vacations? When I'd signed on, it had been enough to love teaching and working with kids, and to me that still seemed enough. But increasingly, nothing less than executive-level organizational and multitasking skills—decidedly not my forte—would satisfy this district.

Marianne listened and counseled patiently. I longed to repay in kind, to give our relationship the time it deserved. But instead we suffered further stress as my weight climbed, Dr. Wesley kept adding meds, and Marianne's friends and family warned that she would soon have a very sick man on her hands. I ate healthy food, but way too much. The craving was incessant.

In June, with two years to go, my annual physical confronted me with unrelieved starkness: full-blown diabetes and hypertension barely controlled by meds, along with a host of related conditions. Dr. Wesley piled on yet more prescriptions.

That evening I set to sorting old pills, new pills, pinks, greens, blues, and whites, round ones and square ones—when a psychic heave grabbed me and sat me down, sobered and grim. Absolutely no way would this go two more years. I yearned to stalk into the principal's office and proclaim my resignation, effective yesterday. Eventually a calmer mood took over.

But the way was finally clear. I'd work one more year

and retire at fifty-nine. By combining vacations and accumulated sick leave with sheer relief, I could survive it. It would cost—a quick calculation warned of a further 15 percent cut in income over the big one I'd already adjusted to, but none of that mattered. My health was no longer for sale.

I can't say the last year was easy, given burnout, medical worries, and ever-mounting accountability. Bilingual ed was gone, but since I spoke Spanish, I got the limited-English speakers, held to the same standards as the fluent speakers. Instant grade-level English readers, courtesy of magic.

"There are only two variables that determine a student's success," the principal informed me one day. "And of these, teacher effectiveness is primary."

"I'll try my best. And what is the other variable?"

"Minor student factors." He waved it off.

It turned out these included home environment, behavior, intelligence, language—details like that. It was stunning to discover that the routine proficiency of a routine teacher could simply take aim at reality and vaporize it. With a straight face I thanked the principal for this fascinating new perspective.

At last, I had come to terms with my job. Years of grateful parents, appreciative fifth-grade teachers, and the thrill of guiding kids had been enough all along to sustain my professional satisfaction. As for the rest, the surest defense against cognitive disconnect was a sense of humor, never before my strong suit. Now for that one long last year, I wielded it freely.

Granted, it could verge on insufferable. When fourth-grade staff development (matrix rubrics) rotated to my room, I posted it as ordered. And caused a ruckus. What was the idea, spelling *staff* with *ph?* That spelling was listed in *Webster's*, I replied, and it was simply a helpful description of the proceedings.

Mostly, though, I trooped on, savoring my time with the kids. Then it was over.

Years of weight lifted as friends marveled at how much more lightly I stepped. Weight also lifted, literally, though it took several years to get it back down and regain my health.

I was smelling roses, smiling at squirrels, and spending plenty of time with family and friends that I'd long neglected. My relationship with Marianne developed into all I'd hoped for, with movies, family events, and trips to Yosemite. Though we did separate eventually, it was due to honest differences rather than job craziness.

At odd moments I would shudder at some flashback and acknowledge how closely I'd courted disaster. Had I insisted on pursuing work for two more years until I was sixty, almost certainly something awful would have struck me down.

I downgraded my expired Accord to a Civic, and it drove beautifully. As epic trips to New Zealand faded, I replaced them with another kind of exploration: checking out volunteer work that would help preserve the beauty of nature while drawing on my teaching skills.

By now I have worn several volunteer hats and made fabulous new friends. The pay's a little slim, but I couldn't ask for greater satisfaction, nor feel more gratitude for the self-respect that evolved out of that simple date years ago.

A BREATH OF LIFE

•

by Tamsen Butler

MY DAUGHTER AND I WERE ALWAYS ON THE GO. AROUND the time she was six weeks old, she and I had become quite a team; if we weren't at the mall, the zoo, the art museum, the park, or some other worthwhile distraction then we were at home, twiddling our thumbs, nervously awaiting the next trip out. Of course, she was probably completely happy being home, but it seemed to me that we should always be out and doing something. If I didn't pack her day with activities, her cognitive and physical development would surely suffer, wouldn't it? Consequently, I was one of those moms who enrolled an eight-week-old in organized play classes.

Nineteen months later, along came my son. I envisioned us seamlessly dashing from activity to activity every day, just as I had always done with his older sister. We were going to be the busiest trio in town. My son, on the other hand, wasn't quite up to our hectic pace.

My son has always had a bit of a problem with breathing. Whenever he gets a cold, his breathing starts to sound crispy and his oxygen levels start to drop. I must have sat through a dozen different appointments with a dozen different specialists who gave a dozen different diagnoses: respiratory syncytial virus, asthma, bronchitis, enlarged adenoids, and my personal favorite: "That's just how he sounds." One of the main concerns I brought up at each appointment was my fear that he was too sick to go out and about. I dreaded the idea of the three of us sitting at home and missing out on all the social interaction and visual stimulation which I was convinced the kids needed in order to someday grow into brilliant adults.

Last winter, my son's breathing got worse. He sounded so crispy and loud when he breathed that people in grocery stores would stop me to ask in horrified voices if he was okay. Sometimes I would stand outside his room at night while he slept and I would just cry. What else could I do? He sounded so horrible that no matter how many times the doctors told me he was fine, I could not help but feel as though I was failing him as a mother by not single-handedly curing his health problems.

Eventually, his breathing got so bad that he was having trouble staying awake during the day and had to be admitted to the local children's hospital. He was fifteen months old at the time and, while at the doctor's office with my husband, his oxygen levels had dropped so low that he needed an oxygen tank for the ride to the hospital. I don't know if most people have ever seen an oxygen line strapped to the face of a fifteen-month-old, but the memory of it still makes my heart pound.

My husband called me on my cell phone while I was at the grocery store to let me know that my son was getting admitted. I dashed home to drop off the groceries and grab a few items for the overnight stay at the hospital, then drove like a madwoman to the doctor's office. I made it just in time to load my son and myself into the ambulance and take the ride to the hospital. I clutched my son in one arm while I used my other arm to balance my laptop bag on the bench. I brought my computer with me because I am a freelance writer, and I had a few projects looming that were due soon. The thought of missing a deadline just didn't seem like an acceptable prospect.

Incidentally, I was also enrolled in college classes fulltime and was additionally running a local theater production. As always, I was scheduled beyond my capacity, and one of the thoughts in my mind was how to take care of my son while also finishing my writing jobs, completing my class assignments, and not missing a rehearsal for the play.

After my son was admitted and all the initial tests and evaluations were done, he fell asleep out of utter exhaustion. I stared at him, quietly crying so as not to wake him, and once I was composed enough, I sighed and turned on my laptop. I had a long night ahead of me; I figured everything would undeniably spiral out of control if I ignored my duties for one night. I worked long into the night, periodically stopping to assist the respiratory therapist with my son's breathing treatments.

One night in the hospital led to another, then another, and yet another. My son was not getting the oxygen he needed, and he was to remain in the hospital until he could breathe on his own. The first couple of nights I worked feverishly on my laptop while my son slept. It began to dawn on me eventually, however, that I had put myself in a ridiculous position. When had working become more important than my own well-being? I realized that the ambulance ride to the hospital had been a metaphor for my life—instead of clutching my son with only one arm I should have had both arms wrapped around him, embracing him like only a comforting mother can do.

The third night in the hospital I got angry with myself. My son was in the hospital, and I was a fool. I hadn't thought to notify my editors because turning work in late simply seemed unacceptable. I didn't tell my professors what was going on because I didn't want it to seem like I was complaining about my situation. I still attended the theater rehearsals while my husband stayed at the hospital with my son, because I didn't want to let all the actors down.

Something about that third night in the hospital opened my eyes. The doctors were optimistic that my son would head home in the morning, and although my initial reaction was relief that we could get back to life as it was before the hospitalization, I knew that something had to change. Since when was any job or any school assignment more important than putting my full concentration toward my son? Furthermore, why had I allowed myself to skip much-needed sleep in the hospital in order to get my work done? Looking back now, it seems to me that while my son was sleeping, I should have been sleeping too, not working on the computer in an attempt to meet all my deadlines as though everything was normal. Here comes the big realization: I am not Superwoman.

The hospital stay was cathartic. My son was released on the fourth day and hasn't been hospitalized since. His breathing condition was finally properly diagnosed as laryngomalacia, and we know that he is expected to outgrow his crispy breathing in a few years. I have greatly modified my work ethic; no longer do I accept work assignments to simply pad my résumé or bring in more money. I accept work now that I find compelling and meaningful. What a difference this has made in my life! Initially my decision to take in less work resulted in less money, but surprisingly enough, once I started doing work I enjoyed, the jobs started pouring in. Now I make more money than I did before. Isn't it funny how these things work out?

Something else changed in our family as a result of the hospitalization. The doctors warned us to keep my son away from other kids for the entire duration of the winter. With my affinity for filling our days with activity after activity, the thought of staying home through the whole winter terrified me. Truthfully, the first week was rough. I longed to pack up the kids and go to the gym or to a playgroup. Eventually, however, I began to realize that there is something truly beautiful about a family being able to spend time at home and just enjoy each other's company. I think the entire process has made me a far better mother, and I know it has enhanced my children's lives. Now they know how to amuse themselves at home in a simple way, without a constant barrage of activity.

The hospital stay and subsequent social hibernation we experienced prompted us to simplify our lives in other ways too. It was as if the whole event made us take a hard look at the way we lived our lives. We took a look around our house and started wondering, "Do we really need all this stuff?" We began packing up toys that the kids didn't play with anymore, the clothes that we didn't wear, and all the other things that were doing nothing more than taking up space in the house, and sent them off to Goodwill.

All the while, we tried to explain to our daughter what we were doing. I wasn't sure if she understood what was going on, but she seemed to be taking it relatively well that a good portion of her toys were getting bagged up and sent off to people who could use them—at least as well as a preschooler can take something like that. A few weeks later, though, she happened to rip a piece of clothing, and I told her that she wouldn't be able to wear it anymore. Her response was, "Maybe we can give it to charity." What a wonderful moment for a mother! Although she didn't understand that only serviceable stuff is sent off to charity, she did realize that when we didn't need something anymore, we sent it to people who could use it. I couldn't have been prouder.

There is no reason to dash from one organized activity to the next. There is no reason to fill a house with tons of toys. There is something innately beautiful about just *being*. I truly feel as though my children were blessed by this transformation within our family, and I know for a fact that I was blessed. Simplified life has come as a great relief to me and to my family.

Discovering the

Sanity Within

■

FOREST SOLITAIRE

•

by Andrew Vietze

WAS THIS OSPREY A SIGN? AS I SAT AND WATCHED IT trace circles in the sky above my office, its wings wide and floating, I began to think so. This fish hawk has always been my favorite bird, instantly transporting me to my grandmother's big old saltwater farm where we've camped every summer for more than thirty years. The property is a long, fifty-acre peninsula, and as many as six ospreys at a time can be seen fishing in the tidal river that surrounds us as we gather at the Fourth of July. As a boy, I learned to mimic their high-pitched whistle while I ran around with my cousins. Because it's a family property far from any road, we could range at will, the kind of freedom adults rarely get to feel.

I couldn't help but look up from my desk and watch this particular bird, flying in graceful arcs above our building. For much of the year he'd be there, crying his raptor cry, as if imploring me outside. I'd sit bound to my chair and stare longingly through the glass, remembering what it was like to run around without any walls, without anything overhead but the sky. The osprey did this for years, and eventually it forced my hand.

I quit.

The decision wasn't an easy one. Was I being too

selfish? Perhaps even irresponsible? Here I was, a married adult with a baby on the way and a mortgage to pay. But a miserable mortgage-bound soon-to-be father. I had a good job at a highly regarded magazine; in fact I'd recently been made managing editor, so the money was fine for small-town Maine, and I had a benefits package that would care for me and my new kid. It just wasn't enough, wasn't ever quite right. I'd done everything I could at the magazine after almost ten years, and I couldn't enter the building without my head dropping a bit.

The whole reason I wanted to become a writer in the first place was to live life as an adventure, to live outside the boxes—office buildings, societal requirements. To avoid the nine-to-five, the computer, the phone, the necktie (a colleague and I called it the Daily Noose). Each morning, though, I'd trudge upstairs to my desk and go through the paces while staring out the window. I didn't care about the money. Life was always more important than that.

So I quit.

I had done everything right since college, placing my Edward Abbey and Jack Kerouac fantasies to the rear in favor of paying off student loans. (There's no way Kerouac was an indentured servant to Columbia the way I was to Clark University.) I had a respectable, indeed, sought-after job. I had a nice old white clapboard house in a sweet river valley town and two cars in the driveway. And I'd finally paid off those loans.

So I quit.

As a child there were five things I wanted to be when I grew up, each equal to the others, each a certainty. I wanted to write. Fight fires. Play pro soccer. Be a rock star. And I'd done them all in some fashion. I'd written for a wide variety of magazines. I joined my local fire department and literally bled for it. I played men's league soccer and we were champs four years running at the Maine Sports Complex (0–30 league). I'd put out three records on which I sang or contributed guitar. There was only one thing I had yet to do.

So I quit.

And I became a park ranger. I traded my necktie for a badge, my office for a ranger station, my telephone for a two-way radio, my nine-to-five for a "ten-eight" at seven a.m. Now I not only watch birds—more often than not the loon, another personal favorite—but I live among them in a 200,000-acre park. Every morning I see the sun come up over Maine's highest mountain—some say the first rays to hit the entire country—and watch as it turns the face of my pond into blinding crystal. I see the woods shake off the night and come awake and the fish begin to jump in their great basin. I see campers rise and greet the day with the kind of excitement that only a day away from work in a beautiful setting brings.

The governor who gave these spectacular, storied lands to the State of Maine did so with the proviso that they must be kept forever wild. So not only do I not have to answer phones, there isn't one for miles. No computers, of course, because there's no electricity for miles either.

And I love it. I love my badge. I love my truck. I love my duty station. I love hiking the trails. I love being outside every day no matter the weather. Sharing porch time with the regulars among my campers. Paddling my canoe on the pond at dusk. Working with my hands. Learning to build cabins, reading the landscape and the seasons, joking with Unit 67. Having stand-offs with bobcats, which screech like a horror movie. Chasing down evildoers like Dudley Do-Right. Responding to emergencies. Being part of a grand Maine tradition—and a singular park that's a national treasure. Showing people how important and necessary wild places are.

I distinctly remember telling my sister when I was about five years old—my boy's age now—that I wanted to be a park ranger. And now a friend calls me Ranger Danger. I love it.

It isn't all easy, though, sacrifice and compromise being defining conditions of adulthood. I typically, in the words of a fellow ranger, play nine holes every day. Which is to say I dutifully scrub as many outhouses. (My mom laughs that I went to a fine college and got a degree in English and history only to clean toilets; she jests, though, and completely understands the appeal of park life.) When you do it every day, fighting the forces of feces isn't as onerous as it may sound, and it's a very small price to pay for the privilege of living here.

Park rangers certainly aren't in it for the money—I had jobs that paid more fifteen years ago in college—but I've been able to augment my monthly income with all the writing I can get done at night when I'm off duty. The salary is a lot different than the one I gave up to take this job, and I bought my house when I was making that kind of money. There are months when simply paying the mortgage is a challenge. I have to work every day of the week in the summer in order to sustain the lifestyle. Both cars in our household have over 200,000 miles on them now. Property taxes are a killer.

I occasionally have to deal with difficult people, which isn't exactly a favorite—rangers spend a fair amount of time telling people what they're not allowed to do. (I'm constantly bemused at being looked at by park visitors as some sort of authority figure—I got into this because I'm a nature lover, a punk-rock kid, because of *Desert Solitaire* and *The Dharma Bums*, not because of some innate desire to be a lawman. I think that's true of most park rangers.)

The hours are long. The bugs in the North Woods of June are so ferocious it's almost comical, and I've become a weary soldier in a dragged-out war against the mice in my cabin. Appalachian Trail hikers smell. I have to do more paperwork than you might imagine. I missed most of the last World Cup.

And without a doubt, the worst aspect is that each summer I spend a couple days a week away from my wife and son. Being a freelance writer allows me to be home all the time when I *am* home, but for twenty-something weeks, I'm not. Which is hard on all of us, perhaps most of all my little boy, known to my fellow rangers as "Unit Point Five." (He got this name when I was Unit 5.) He and my wife both love the park, though, and they understand its importance to me.

We make it work. If nothing else, it's an adventure. My son gets to spend his formative years in one of the most beautiful places in the country, and to learn a self-sufficiency and resourcefulness that is so often lost in our culture. He gets to see that happiness is not made from the things you buy and bring with you but rather from life and love and the adventure they bring.

Despite all of these challenges, it's far and away the best job I've ever had. At this point, I'd even rather be a ranger than a rock star. I don't regret in the slightest saying goodbye to my old job, its ways and its wages, its fancy title and prestige, though I do miss the people. I don't miss the phone, the television, the Internet. It was the right choice, at the right time in my life.

Because I make my own schedule for much of the year, and have a lot of free time due to the quietude of the park, my creativity has exploded. I've written a novel about these same woods 150 years earlier, and am halfway through a screenplay (about a park ranger, natch). I have a nonfiction book under way, and I've written many new songs for my band's next record. I read and exercise more than I ever do in the off-season.

If I have my druthers, I'll be in these woods for years. A park ranger until I retire—and beyond. I've found the color of my parachute and it's forest green.

You might say I've gone to the birds.

IGNORING *WALDEN*

•

by Katherine Hauswirth

T
O PAY THE BILLS, I WRITE AND EDIT MEDICAL EDUCA-
tion materials. To pay my spirit, I write essays that reflect on nature and an attitude of simplicity. When people
hear of my love for nature writing and my attraction to a
simpler existence, they often recommend the book *Walden* by Henry David Thoreau.

As a writer, it is embarrassing to admit that I don't
much like Henry David Thoreau. Every nature book I
pick up alludes to *Walden*, and I've read quotes by Thoreau that are singularly brilliant. Despite the reputation
that precedes the book and its author, twice I've picked
up *Walden* and twice I've found myself annoyed by the
flowery language and by Thoreau's entitled-sounding, all
or nothing, breakaway attitude toward simple living. I
am the first to admit that part of my anti-Walden impulse is just plain jealousy. I have fantasies of living solo
in a cabin and writing my opus (although I would prefer
not having to build the cabin). But there is more to my
self-imposed exile from Walden Pond than green-eyed
envy.

Radical simplicity—you know, the quit your job, grow
your own food, live off the grid type of existence—works
for some. But it scares most of us. It scares some of us so

much that we even shy away from not so radical simplicity, where the move toward a simpler existence can mean very gradually weaning ourselves from the comforting teat of complacency while we awaken to the natural world. The start of this personal growth can be nothing more than happenstance—no manifesto involved. My first steps toward simplicity were more like stumbles in the dark.

In the crowded Long Island, New York suburb where I grew up, people still pay top dollar for the privilege of commuting, crowds, and traffic. Green lawns, new cars, and fashionable clothing ranked pretty high in the culture of my youth. I might still be on the Island if it weren't for a random job offer in Connecticut. After a brief search of shoreline towns we knew little about, Tom and I landed in a comparatively rural setting.

Ever so gradually, the clanging in my brain quieted. I stopped adding a half hour (padding for highway and parking problems) to every car trip, stopped calculating mortgage refinance rates in my head. I started caring less about how I compared with the neighbors. I resurrected the young poet who had gone silent at adolescence and walked the hilly, curved roads that meandered along the coast. I felt satisfied with our humble apartment, the view of the forest outside our back window. Things that felt necessary before now seemed extraneous. Less clutter, physical and psychic, turned into more peace. I started to recognize the power in every choice. Decisions to simplify, though not conscious at first, fanned out from there.

Leaving the field of nursing was another unexpected

departure that cleared my head and simplified my existence. Being a nurse had been a childhood dream, helping people a sacred priority, but I gradually realized that I was exhausting my energies in a system that didn't respect my values. A firsthand witness to treatment decisions driven by insurance and corporate greed, I was drained and disillusioned. I felt suffocated by my choices, backed up against a dead end of disappointment. This was what I had studied so hard for, this was what I had talked about ad infinitum, this was what I had done for over a decade. One day I talked to a nurse who had purchased a bed-and-breakfast after twenty years of nursing, having decided that two decades of selfless service was enough. I felt the proverbial lightbulb glowing above my head. I could leave nursing? I could do something else? My mind and soul leaped at the possibility. Looking back, this was my first major resistance to the *shoulds* that crowded my brain.

I am no Thoreau. I doubt I will ever find myself alone in a cabin for more than a few days. Compared with Thoreau's quest, my changes have been more timid, more gradual, and more accidental. But still, both my move away from suburbia and my rejection of my nursing career were departures from some very comfortable zones, and it would have been easier, at least in the short term, to avoid those choices. Each transition, though difficult at first, reflected my becoming more in tune with who I really was. I learned the first tenet of simple living: to think and act on one's own. It feels good to live beyond *musts* and *shoulds*, to break from the status quo. My attraction to "voluntary simplicity" is an outgrowth of this gradual breaking away, of reappraising what is normal, what is enough for me, what I need to feel satisfied.

When I began to read about others who sought life beyond the treadmill of expectation, my explorations were isolated from action. I wanted to immerse myself in nature, but I didn't want to get into environmentalism. I wanted a less commercial perspective, but I didn't reduce my trips to the store. Only recently did I connect my disdain for material and mental clutter with what it represents: a turning away from any habit that obscures my deepest, truest priorities. I also started to connect my personal actions with a larger picture. I take pleasure in every opportunity to make decisions, knowing that each one ripples out beyond me, if only in small ways, to the world at large.

In truth, I am still in the stage where I am mostly thinking. I am not a vegetarian yet, but I am eating less meat and exploring the next step (fish only). I haven't led any protests, but I have written to the government about our energy and foreign relations policies. I haven't disposed of all my possessions, but I am increasingly likely to put off a new purchase and to share my wealth.

Observation is important to my lifestyle, and I reap tons of satisfaction from considering what's before me, recognizing meaning and beauty within the seemingly mundane world. I wait for the wren who naps in my porch eaves every spring. I rejoice in the nature trail that's hidden just beyond the highway, in the wriggly worms that my son Gavin scoops up from the asphalt after a storm. It's not just nature, although nature is primary. It is also finding an inspiring book among a lack-luster garage sale selection or bagging up clothing I no longer need for donation. Countless small things like these bring me pleasure.

In exploring simplicity discussion forums online, I ran into an anti-status-quo faction that had become a new status quo in the narrower world of that group. They criticized people for buying a new washing machine or questioned whether an eager new simplicity seeker really needed that consignment shop trip. These were the deprivation-proud radicals who insisted that simplicity was an all-or-nothing commitment.

On one extreme of the simple-living spectrum are the territorial types who feel the need to surpass others, who equate ambivalence with weakness. On the other are magazines trying to convince us that scaling down requires more purchases: we have to go out and stock up on wholesome, charming, simplicity-related supplies. Sometimes I want to cut through the media babble and be more of an uncompromising idealist; sometimes I want stacks of new boxes and shelves for organizing my kitchen. I can be attracted to either impulse, depending on my mood. But what really feels right is striving for independent thought and shunning programmed activity of any kind. I believe that we can all find ways to lighten our stress as well as our imprint on the earth, but like all change this will happen only in fits and starts, the sum of our own individual paces.

For the moment, my most steady contribution toward living simply is my blog. It reflects my gradual and often tenuous grasp on free-thinking and thoughtful action. I try to provide some food for thought, both for myself and my readers. We need the real (practical advice for paring down, strategies to avoid "complexity traps") as well as the ideal (big thoughts on humankind, nature, and spirituality; lofty ambitions).

Which brings me back to Walden Pond. Thoreau leaned heavily toward the idealist side of the road, but maybe I've come down too hard on him. I don't think he chastised those who had not, in fact, built themselves a cabin and left their family behind in town. He did admit that he didn't know it all, as in his famous first lines:

> I went to the woods because I wished to live deliberately, to front only the essential facts of life, and see if I could not learn what it had to teach, and not, when I came to die, discover that I had not lived.

I didn't go to the woods, at least not to live. But I am mulling over the very same sorts of things here in my basement office. I return upstairs after this latest contemplation, registering the wave of warmth that greets my emergence from the uninsulated depths of my home. Shaking off the chill, I think about it again. Maybe I'll give *Walden* another try.

LOSING AND WINNING

•

by Galen Warden

AROUND 1990 MY HUSBAND SUCCUMBED TO MAJOR depression and just stopped working. I had to support the eight of us—we had six young children. In the months that followed it became apparent that, without either a college degree or full-time work experience, I would not earn enough to support us sufficiently.

We began to sell our belongings. We received food from a local church soup kitchen, and hand-me-downs for my older kids from neighbors, as I continued to look for work. Plus we began to look for a low-cost rental, awaiting our inevitable eviction. Picture a financial domino effect—complete with jumps, flips, and cascades. But even then I was certain that this period of our lives held its own lessons and would always be remembered as a very meaningful journey.

As we sold our belongings and began to scale down our lives, I felt a sense of liberty I did not expect. We had already spent a fair amount of time without a television because I could not bear to see my children sit longingly in front of toy commercials. Of course they watched it at friends' houses. I told them I didn't hate television, but I wanted their time at home to be spent doing, not wishing. We had a big roll of white butcher paper and plenty of crayons, markers, and paint. We had Legos and Lincoln Logs and blocks. We had guitars and tambourines and keyboards. My husband was a musician and I am an artist, so creative equipment was readily available to them. Fast-forward—today they are all artists and musicians either for their jobs or as a hobby.

We enjoyed our creativity at home, but getting out of the house was important too. The problem there, again, was that we could not afford the normal entertainments: movies, local carnivals, or amusement parks. Instead I discovered that one of the coolest things to do without money is "window shop." I'd take my girls to a fancy store, like Bloomingdale's, and we'd try on fur coats! Window shopping was excellent therapy and recreation, plus it was educational. So much can be learned by not purchasing a thing or spending a dime.

It's helpful to remember that shopping in the traditional sense is very different and much more stressful. You have to select the right thing. Does it go with my other stuff? Is it appropriate for my personal style? Does it fit? Does it match? Can I afford it? Should I go for cheap, or splurge? Plus you have to limit yourself to stores likely to carry items that conform to your taste, needs, and budget.

Window shopping reduces all of this stress. You can window shop in any store that will allow you in. Money is no object. The style doesn't have to suit your taste. Ponder stuff you'd never put in your home.

It's really quite amazing when you consider the millions of items for sale and the millions of different people buying them. Ask yourself what might have been in the mind of the manufacturer. Why did they choose to make this item? They must have imagined the perfect customer for it. You can picture the most sophisticated, or the most vain, people needing to pamper themselves with items of pure luxury—completely unnecessary extravagances whose qualities, details, or ornamentations augment an everyday object, simply to make it appeal to their sense of entitlement. If someone has to have the very most expensive one, then certainly someone will figure out how to make one of those that are expensive. You can eye each item—whether a teacup, a coat, or a jewel—and paint an imaginary portrait of the character who would *have* to have that one!

To add a sense of history, and often irony, antique stores are great. There you can not only enjoy imagining who might pay $200 for a fountain pen, you can try to picture its humble origins at 25¢ in the stationery store in 1920. This adds a wonderful twist. Antique items may represent a new technology for their time— the very latest thing—and with the perspective of history we recognize that one day our own modern things will be out-dated curiosities also. Vintage clothing may show shades of modern styles, back around again. And vintage photos are the perfect window on families who may have been similar to our own ancestors. We can look into their eyes and imagine what that day may have been like, having their photo taken after a long horse-and-buggy ride into town.

Window shopping is a healthy adventure for well-behaved children six to twelve years or a little older. They are still young enough to have their values shaped, to

appreciate that everyone doesn't have the same taste, and
to recognize that stuff is just stuff—and that very little is
essential stuff. Every item in every store merely has the
purpose of providing revenue to those who present it.
There is no need to buy it. However, it is amazing how
items themselves are somehow infused with the spirit of
those desperate to possess them. There is a strange satisfaction in conjuring up that sensation in ourselves, recognizing it for what it is, and then watching it evaporate.
Our power to overcome the siren call of an item that
beckons, "Owning me will improve you," is a good skill to
hold on to throughout life. You will own your things.
They will not own you.

At this moment, having lost everything those many
years ago, I can gratefully say that I can afford to give
regularly to the charities of my choice—Habitat for
Humanity and the Salvation Army, among others—understanding that it is often someone just like me (because
once it was me) who loses everything and needs a hand
for a while. I can also happily say that, although I have
more stuff than I had at that time, none of it, not a single
thing, has the power it once had to hurt me. The threat of
losing my things was a painful feeling that won't be repeated.

My primary goal through those difficult times was to
fiercely guard my kids against any negative impact from
our situation. I was determined that it would be an opportunity to create better priorities and perspective. I
could use this experience to instill a sense of self-worth
in them that was totally unrelated to status and to teach
them empathy for others they would encounter in their

futures. What a gift! We sang, we drew, we played, we window shopped. With the exception of my husband, who took a few years to get better, we worked to remain happy, playful people.

Since those days I've become a successful career woman and own my own home. The value of learning that "stuff is just stuff," the liberty of having nothing to lose and reveling consciously in that freedom, is the richest reward that one could gain from the exorcism of losing it all.

The Sweetness in You

I know how fragile life is.
Breath preciously taken in and carefully given out again.
You are a living rhythm of earth's waves, tides, seasons.

Your heart, a delicate flower
Opening and closing its valves within a golden cage of
*   bones.*
A miracle each moment. Every time.

I adore your skin, its intricate capillaries peaking through
And blue veins like ribbons
Feeding every inch of you.

I fully acknowledge the mercy of life:
The gifts of cloud and sea and field
To our unworthy eyes and hands.

Water from the well.
Sun on the sand.
Life is good! So good. So good.

And things—the stuff of society:
Jewels and sweaters and heels and purses,
Lamps and radios and rubber tires . . .
All of it I appreciate more than you could understand.
The hands that made. The minds that planned.
The dreams that originated every wish that became
A thing to use, to want, to have.

From the silver thimble my great-grandmother used
To the gleaming granite countertop I polish with joy—
All of the things of life are sweet.

But none is as precious as warm skin with fine hairs
*   and freckles.*
. . . The flower of the heart opening and closing its valves.
. . . Blue ribbons coursing through you.
. . . The breath of life taken in . . . most of it given back.

Be life with me!
Even more fragile than things.
Be precious gift of warm blood and bones.

Be aware with me
That the things we create wither
As easily as life escapes the delicate skin of the dead.

But as long as rosy cheeks flush with hope,
The joy of you is complete without a thing.

Let them take the house.
Let the items I have treasured slip away . . .
Bring me your splendor caged in bones,
That glorious mind that sparks with light.
The life of you . . . mine for the giving of mine to.

Nothing extra needed, dear.
No thing, but the sweetness in you
Which decorates the sweetness in me
Better than any thing.

—*Galen Warden*

DOWNWARD MOBILITY:
HOW I STEPPED
OFF THE LADDER

•

by Brian Simkins

$\mathcal{I}$ PUT MY FOOT ON THE FIRST RUNG OF THE CORPORATE ladder when I was twenty-seven. It seemed to me that most responsible and contributing members of society do this sort of thing, so I ignored the fact that I didn't really want retail management to be my lifelong vocation. The job was available, I was qualified, and the money was good.

My wife and I, like most young couples, had struggled to establish ourselves financially, and this new job opportunity seemed as good as any. In hindsight, I can see that taking this position was an attempt to catch that elusive wave that we call the American Dream. It never occurred to me to be concerned about the fact that I had no innate passion for the job. I showed up every day and worked with a sense of urgency because, well, that's what you do when you want to get your foot onto the next rung of that ladder.

Work ethic is a curious thing. I have a hard time identifying exactly where mine came from. I would like to think that I am driven to work hard because I absorbed some of the wisdom demonstrated by all of the hard-working people who have had some influence in my life. Honestly, it could just be an unhealthy need to please people. Regardless of the source, I have learned that if you do work hard, show up on time, and follow directions, you just might end up running the place someday. And I did.

Promoted several times in rapid succession, it didn't take long for me to start feeling that I was pretty important. The best thing was that, with each promotion, I got a raise that I could feel was making a difference in what the corporation defined as my "quality of life." I was, for the first time, making what most would consider good money. I felt that I was providing for my family and fulfilling that drive men seem to have in our culture to be breadwinners. Having gotten married while still in college, my wife and I were now grateful not to be subsisting on pancakes anymore. I had finally figured out the timing of the wave that drives corporate success, and I was riding it pretty well.

Sometimes, the changes in our lives are obvious. When you start having kids, you feel the impact immediately. If a loved one or a parent dies, the scope and flavor of your life changes forever. These transformations happen in an instant. You can mark a specific time and date on the calendar and know that from that moment on, your life will be different.

Other changes have a habit of sneaking up on you, though, when you are busy paying attention to something else. I wasn't anticipating this brand of change. I wasn't aware. Completely caught up in enjoying our newfound prosperity, we didn't see the transformations coming. These changes were the sneaky kind.

Slowly, as though through a thick morning fog, I began to notice that a few things in my life that had always been well established were no longer so stable. The circumstances of life were changing in more than a few disconcerting ways and, as a result, I was changing as well. It was subtle at first.

We began to notice that even though we now had the extra cash to do some of things we had always wanted to do, it seemed that we never had the time. I had to work nearly every weekend until eleven p.m. On weekdays I was up and gone by four a.m. and when I was home I was less than helpful. I began bowing out of commitments that I had previously made, simply because I was exhausted. I would disappear into my job for weeks at a time, without contacting friends or family, when things got stressful or busy at work.

I couldn't sleep at night because I was lying in bed trying to play out the next day in my head. The problems of my employees began to wear on me as I realized that I couldn't remain professionally detached forever. In the midst of all these changes, I also learned some harsh realities about the corporate mindset. As I came to understand that I was no more than a renewable commodity—meant to be sucked dry and then discarded—I tried to hang on even tighter. I learned that it is hard to hang on to the corporate ladder when your hands are already full. Suddenly, the changes were no longer subtle.

Last July, we flew to upstate New York to spend some time with family and to indulge in a well-earned vacation. As tired and ready for a vacation as I was, I couldn't relax. I was on a quiet beach at Lake Ontario more than one thousand miles away from any responsibilities, and all I could think about was my job. I sat in the sun stewing over how much extra work there would be when I got back.

The dream had ceased being a dream. Its nightmare grip on me was so tight that I couldn't step away from it for even a week. Somewhere along the way, I had developed an image in my mind of what a driven corporate professional looked like, and that image gripped me mentally, emotionally, and even physically. Finally, after everyone on my family vacation gave up and stopped asking me what was wrong, I began to talk my way through it. After a few more days, and some good conversation with loved ones, I began to see that this escape to the lake was more than a little vacation. Sitting in the sun, examining the ladder that I was trying so hard to climb, I realized that this trip was going to change everything.

I remember learning an elementary school lesson explaining why horses that pulled wagons through the mountains wore blinders. The leaders of the wagon trains placed leather straps over the horses' eyes so that they could only see straight ahead. If they had been able to see the sharp precipice on which they were walking, the horses would have either stopped dead in their tracks or spooked and run right off the edge. Blind to the danger, though, the unsuspecting horses would charge right up harrowing mountain switchbacks. Duped into believing they were safe, they could focus on their masters' wishes. Blinded by repeated promises of more promotions and an even higher "quality of life," I realized that I had been racing along a precipice that had no bottom.

It was on the last day of that quiet vacation, far away from the everyday stress of management, that I decided to quit my job. I don't think I ever would have done it if my family hadn't been so insistent that something just wasn't right with me. Standing on the shore of Lake Ontario, I realized that with every promotion, I would have to give the company a lot more of my time and another little piece of my soul. My mother-in-law finally made me realize just how badly I needed the change. She told me that I wasn't the same person she used to know. It seemed, she said, that I had grown harder, more calloused. That was one of those sneaky changes I didn't see coming.

From there, it didn't take long to make a decision. This was not what I wanted to spend the next thirty-five years doing. I knew it would eventually destroy my marriage, my relationships, and my spirit. The time and emotional effort that my job required were no longer worth the cost. My wife and I decided together that the time had come to make a change.

Our plane touched down in Chicago at about eight-thirty on a Sunday night. When the captain announced that we could turn on our cellular phones, I cringed to see that I had accumulated a mass of voicemails over the course of the week. One problem after another would demand my attention from the moment I picked up my baggage. I knew I had to address the issues that were waiting for me in the heat of that moment, but I also knew that I had one additional call to place. After dealing with all of the pressing issues, I hit the speed dial button that linked my cell phone to my boss. "Meet me tomorrow morning for breakfast," I said. "We need to talk."

I had a professor in college who always encouraged us, when the semester was winding down, to "Finish well." His admonitions to avoid "short-timer's syndrome" and to press on while giving our very best was sound advice. I had always made an effort to carry those words into my professional career. When I walked out of the door, thirty days after meeting my boss for breakfast, my head was high, my smile was bright, and my spirit was free.

I knew that I had finished well and done the best that I could by my employer and my employees. I knew that I had taken a huge step toward transforming the shape of my family's future, and I knew that I was now free to find a vocation that would allow me to really live in this world, not just exist in it while the planet spun around me.

A friend asked me recently if I could weigh the pros and cons of the decision I made. Certainly, there are both, and some are more tangible than others. I can point to concrete pros, such as being able to spend the weekends with my family and friends instead of working and such as being around in the morning to have coffee with my wife. I think, however, that I find the biggest benefits in the intangibles. The dramatic reduction in my stress level has made me more emotionally available to everyone in my life, I can sleep at night, and I'm not exhausted all the time.

I'd be lying if I said we didn't miss that income sometimes. We've scaled back our standard of living and there have been some frustrating moments. We've had to politely decline some social outings simply because the checkbook doesn't stretch quite as far anymore. Through it all, though, my wife and I can look at each other and honestly say that we chose this scaled-back version of life over the alternative. We have learned that time together doesn't have to cost anything, and that time apart costs too much.

As of this writing, about eight months have passed since my last day in corporate America. I have started a small, but surprisingly feisty, freelance writing business. It allows me to work from home, and I am able to do something that I love. The absence of a corporate ladder here seems odd at times. When it comes to writing, a few get rich and famous, which is more a matter of being in the right place at the right time. Skill alone often isn't enough to get your foot in the door. I am humbled by the knowledge that there are a number of excellent writers who will never get a big break.

With that knowledge in mind, I am grateful that I am able to make a living in this way at all. Granted, writing is not making us rich, but we are beginning to live again. The income is not always much, but we've decided that it's enough.

'Unstuffing'
One's Life

■

MORE IS LESS:
CONFESSIONS OF A
CLUTTER QUEEN

•

By Liz Milner

EVER NOTICE HOW GLORIOUSLY MESSY NATURE IS? THERE'S mud and sleet and squishy stuff galore and random tricks of light that make your heart just about burst. I've always thought my home should be like that—a place of unlimited abundance. There unexpected juxtapositions of treasure and trash would produce epiphanies; those lightening-flash moments when hidden truths are revealed and one's consciousness is transformed.

What's missing in all the puritanical, hyperorganized, feng shui, simple-life rhetoric is that spontaneity and a touch of randomness are a necessary part of creativity. "Mess for success" was my mantra for most of my adult life. I even wrote a song about my clutter, "Good Enough for Me and All My Debris," to the tune of "Me and Bobbie McGee." A little clutter is fun. What I've learned over the past twenty years of accumulation, however, is that a lot of clutter is just trash.

It started innocently enough. I got a job with a national news organization. Employees were encouraged to help themselves to materials from the promo pile— a seemingly endless supply of just-released books, recordings, magazines, and videos. I love words in all their permutations, so I was in hog heaven. I read books with titles like *The Sexual Politics of Meat*, *How to Become an Innkeeper*, and *Kiss Me, Kill Me.* I had no real interest in these things, but the promos were there and they were free.

I'm broadening my knowledge of the world, I thought, but in truth I was losing focus on the things that really mattered to me. My interests were quickly buried in a humongous pile of stuff that seemed to require endless sorting and arranging. I was so busy with the stacks that I didn't have time to wonder why I never seemed to do anything else or why I couldn't imagine any job but the dead-end one that I held.

The piles represented a source of fossilized fun. Someday, I thought, I'll have the time to go through the stacks and find that tune I wanted to learn. Someday, I thought, I'll get around to drawing the people in that photograph that I clipped five—or was it six?—years ago . . .

"Roads not traveled," that's what the stacks really were. Potential unrealized. Dreams deferred. They were constant reminders that I'd still not written my graphic novel, learned to speak fluent Gaelic, or morphed into a brilliant pastry chef in my spare time.

The stacks began to exert an influence on my financial and social life. Checks and bills would disappear into the piles, sometimes not to be seen for years, with disastrous consequences. I longed to invite friends over, but first I had to tidy up. As the years went by, the tidying took longer and longer: first a couple of hours, then a day, then a weekend of work. When the house was finally in a state to be seen, I was too exhausted to even think of entertaining.

Self-knowledge isn't all it's cracked up to be. I recognized that I didn't own this stuff, the stuff owned me. The solution—setting life goals and throwing out the stuff that didn't contribute to the realization of these goals—seemed too draconian. It would be cutting off possibilities, amputating a part of myself. Besides, I could always look at my mom's piles and promise myself that I'd do something if I ever reached her level of accumulation.

My mom's clutter is the stuff of legend. When she last moved ten years ago, it took the movers three days to empty her three-bedroom apartment. While my clutter is mainly books and recordings, my mom's stuff is imbued with a fetishistic aura. Her apartment is a shrine to objects with high-sounding names like Royal Doulton, Wedgwood, Oreffors, and Belleek. Her walls are crowded with Photographs of the Ancestors and original batiks, watercolors, and other objets d'art. Her chandelier belonged to a president and her elbow-length lace gloves shook hands with the queen of England. All these treasures are scattered willy-nilly around her apartment along with every Book of the Month Club selection since 1985, stacks of magazines, a wide array of craft supplies, and lots of chocolate.

As my mom has aged, she's had to employ numerous helpers who have added their own touches to the chaos. We now have last year's news on every doorknob and a polka-dot granny thanks to the insane house painter who covered the doorknobs with at least three inches of masking tape and newspaper, yet had no qualms about flicking beige paint all over the family portraits. Then there was the maid who had a talent for breaking things. Being an honest woman, she never hid the breakage. She'd carefully arrange the pieces on the nearest shelf. My mom couldn't bear to throw anything away, so the fragments would stay as a sort of "found art" piece that was constantly being augmented by new deposits of china and glass shards.

Mom's storage room is the epicenter of a clutter pile that has been forty years in the making. Objects both precious and junky have been hurled into it until the debris stretches almost to the ceiling. My great clutter epiphany happened there.

A half-open bottle of Tia Maria coffee liqueur had fallen. It leaked and covered books, irreplaceable 78-rpm jazz recordings, and batiks in sticky brown ooze. The ooze had been there so long that a thick layer of silvery dust covered it. It had the sick, greenish sheen of spilled antifreeze.

I remembered how proud the artist had been when we'd purchased her batiks. She'd captured the vibrant light of her little island and the perfect curve of a fisherman's back as he threw his net into the sea. Now, instead of kissing the blue Caribbean, the net swirled into a sea of crud. I looked through the sticky stack of records. There was Josh White performing "I Left a Good Deal in Mobile." I always loved Josh White, but now I wouldn't touch that record with a ten-foot pole—or at least without a pair of rubber gloves.

Here was that unexpected juxtaposition of treasure and trash that produced my epiphany. Alas, it was not the revelation of random objects creating senseless beauty that I'd dreamed of. At that moment, I realized that nature isn't only sunsets and rainbows, it's rot, ruin, and waste. Piling precious objects on top of each other hadn't created more beauty—just irreparable loss.

It struck me then that, like our clutter, our lives don't automatically fall into shape. We need to be stewards to our souls by making the conscious choices that shape and nurture them and by occasionally having the courage to throw out the trash.

REMEMBERING
THE POWER

•

by Jon Myhre

WHEN I WAS THIRTEEN, THE SEED OF MY CAREER IN architecture was planted in fertile soil. It sprouted the first time I saw a small but wondrous house. To my young eyes, everything about it was perfect, from the little roof over the front door providing shelter for those awaiting entry to the windows that framed views of a nearby park. Nothing about the house was overwhelming or redundant.

Rather, every one of its elements was beautiful in a quiet way and graciously accommodating to human use. Initially, the house evoked excitement, since I had never seen anything like it. But soon the excitement morphed into a solid feeling of happiness and well-being. I wanted to live in a place like that and resolved that some day I would.

It was designed and owned by a kindly husband and wife, who were both practicing architects. They were customers on the paper route I was maintaining at the time, so I got to see the interior of their house during my weekly collections. It was as elegant and free of superfluity on the inside as the outside, and I could sense that it made them very happy. Although I wasn't aware of it at the time, experiencing their house—and the effect it had on them—gave me a lesson about the power of simplicity for human fulfillment. Unfortunately, it was a lesson I would forget.

After my first semester in the College of Architecture, memories of that house were eclipsed by the exciting stuff I was learning. I found myself unwilling to part with the multitude of drawings and cardboard models I was producing in my classes. My room began to take on a cluttered atmosphere. Then it got worse. I began to collect things—photographs at first, most of which I took myself. They covered the walls and lay in piles on the floor. Soon added to them were the books and magazines I had no time to read. The floor became a storage space with narrow pathways to my bed and desk.

By graduation time I was married. My librarian wife and I found good jobs, which gave us a fairly large amount of discretionary income. We began to accumulate everything we thought emblematic of our sophistication: hundreds of books, art and travel magazines, framed prints of fine art, hand-thrown pottery, Danish furniture, small pieces of sculpture, exotic masks, and lots of clothes. In addition, I kept most of the stuff I had gathered at school.

At first we had shelves for the books and magazines, plenty of wall space for the pictures and masks, closet space for the clothes, and out-of-the-way flat surfaces for the sculptures. But as we acquired more, everything began to spill over onto the furniture and floor, then into boxes under the carport. Our home had become one big storage unit, with no place to entertain friends. Our social life shrank since we could not reciprocate the dinners and gatherings we attended at others' homes. Old friends began to drift away, yet new ones didn't appear.

Without thinking, we attempted to make up for our lack of a social life by working harder and accumulating more things. There was no shortage of encouragement for this sort of endeavor. Our employers were delighted, and our increasing wealth seemed to gain respect from friends and relations who still kept in contact with us. We were "getting ahead," fulfilling the American dream, weren't we?

We preferred our places of work more than our home, which had become only a place to sleep. Breakfast was grabbed on the way to work, lunch and dinner wolfed down in nearby restaurants. We rarely saw each other, except at night, since we worked in different parts of the city. The kitchen in our home was gathering dust, unused even on Sundays when we ate in more restaurants.

Our marriage suffered. We increasingly blamed each other for what was missing in our lives. My wife accused me of not keeping things repaired and the lawn mowed. I berated her for not taking an interest in keeping the house clean or making an occasional meal. But doing any of those things involved moving boxes of junk and stacks of magazines, tasks too daunting even to contemplate.

In our infrequent but desperate efforts to get rid of some of the clutter, we would madly "go through" things. This usually resulted in a few neater piles of items we simply couldn't part with. To escape it all, we would go on occasional short vacations to the most expensive and exotic resorts we could find. Returning from those places to our mess at home put us in a depression that would last for weeks.

During my wife's first pregnancy we were forced to confront a dilemma—she wanted to continue with her career rather than be a full-time mother, but every prospective nanny we interviewed took one look at our home and declined. When the baby came, my wife had to stay home. Although this initially produced enormous stress, in spite of the love we shared for our beautiful new daughter, it proved to be a blessing in disguise. Because my wife was no longer employed, we were forced to stop our compulsive buying of things that added to the chaos. It was our first step toward a lifestyle of elegant simplicity.

One Sunday, when we were "going through" things, I came across a long-forgotten book on historical Japanese architecture. A full-page photo of a residential interior kicked my memory into overdrive. Although it was totally dissimilar in form, it evoked the same feeling I had experienced long ago when I first saw the architects' house on my paper route. It was like finding a long-lost jewel of enormous value and gave me the direction I needed to help turn our lives around.

The first thing I did, when my wife and baby daughter were spending a week with my wife's parents, was to transform our bedroom. After removing the boxes of books stored under my daughter's crib, I went into my closet and flung out all the clothes I had not worn during the past year. I performed the same operation on my side of the bureau drawers. Of the dozens of pictures and masks on the walls, I kept only two of the best photos, and placed them so that only one could be seen at a time, to preserve their full aesthetic impact.

Then it was time to "go through" the hundreds of books on the shelves covering one entire wall. I removed those we had read and those we would probably never read. There were only about a dozen left, which I put on shelves in the living room. After the bookshelves were removed, I painted the ceiling, walls, and bureau drawers a very soft blue.

To me, the room was transformed into the space of rest and love it was meant to be. I held my breath when my wife saw it for the first time. What would be her reaction? Heretofore, neither of us had changed anything in our home environment without consulting the other. For a long moment there was total silence. Then she turned to me. There were tears in her eyes. I found out, much to my relief, what they meant when she flung her arms around me.

Later on I showed her the large mound of stuff I had taken from the bedroom to the carport and covered with a tarp. I asked her if she'd like to "go through" it. She said, "Let's have a garage sale instead." What we didn't sell we gave to the local library and nearest thrift store. In fact, we had five more garage sales as we went from room to room, repeating what had been done in the bedroom.

With the transformation of our home, good things began to happen—our bickering and alienation disappeared, our health improved, we spent quality time together, our daughter turned into a delightful little handful, we entertained at home regularly, became gourmet cooks, and found a great nanny.

No longer did we use our careers as an escape. We learned to keep them within boundaries that would not impact our family and social life. In short, we worked less and played more. We no longer needed the money required before, even with the added expenses incurred by a daughter and nanny. We rarely ate in restaurants, bought just what we needed, and did not desire expensive vacations, preferring instead the pleasures afforded through family and friends.

We learned to maintain our new lifestyle of elegant simplicity by not allowing anything to accumulate. Bills were paid the day they arrived, catalogues and brochures that came through the mail were either read and acted upon the day they arrived or put in a tray for a week. If they weren't acted upon during that time, they were put in the trash.

Before we purchased anything besides food, we made absolutely sure it had a space within our home. If it was a work of art, like a painting or sculpture, it needed to be seen by itself, not visually encroached upon by anything else. If it was a book, there needed to be available shelf space. If it was an article of clothing, it needed purpose and closet or drawer space available to store it. If it was furniture, it needed to avoid redundancy.

Our living space, like all family living spaces, was not perfect, but to us it was so delightful that sometimes we found ourselves wondering if the architects on my paper route were as happy in their home as we were in ours.

MOVING INTO FOCUS

•

By Stephanie Barton

I'VE MOVED SIX TIMES IN THE PAST TEN YEARS. MY husband's career in the military has taken us around the world, from a scrappy little apartment in New York to a breezy house in Hawaii. While anyone might expect all that moving to cause a lot of stress (of course it did), it eventually helped us streamline our home and really embrace a more minimalist approach to living.

Starting with Nothing

We started in New York, with nothing really. Lee and I lived in a tiny apartment above a restaurant, with wall-to-wall orange carpeting that covered a badly slanted floor. Almost everything we owned was given to us by family or bought at yard sales or auctions. A broken futon served as our couch and we shared a rickety dresser with rose decals that I'd had since I was five. Our nightstands were the trunks Lee had been issued at West Point.

When I was just starting out, I'd visit my father's house and he let me take things I liked for my apartment. My father liked to collect things and after he retired, he rented a booth at an antique market and tried turning his hobby into part-time work. He went to weekly auctions, saying he was buying more merchandise for his shop. But half of it just went into his house, so I figured he wouldn't miss anything that went into mine.

When Lee finished medical school, we were told we were going to Texas. He owed time to the military for West Point and med school and so we headed for San Antonio. It took just a few hours for the movers to box up everything we owned and shove it in the back of a truck.

Despite long discussions about life in the military, I was a little bitter about moving to Texas. I'd always seen myself living in New York—I had a promising career as a graphic designer—and I was sure that San Antonio had nothing to offer. Things started looking up for Texas, though, as we searched for apartments. Everything was new. Everything was bigger. In Texas, our money actually had some power and we could buy some new furniture—a kitchen table, a coffee table—and lots of brand new decorations.

In a year, though, we were headed to Washington, where I landed a job that paid well enough for me to pay off my student loans six years early. Our place in Washington was small, so there was no point buying more furniture for it. Lee and I loved to travel, so we took our extra spending money and started making trips around the country.

Moving on Up

We returned to Texas two years later, and this time we bought a house. It was time to stop living like we were still in college and put some of our money toward decent furniture. Because we still had more moves ahead of us with the military, we couldn't be too whimsical—we needed sturdy furniture that could withstand the careless handling of hired movers. We bought sensibly and splurged on one piece, a large rustic cabinet for our entertainment center.

Now that we had a house and a little more space, our parents had some items of their own they'd been saving as gifts—a china cabinet with years of memorabilia from my in-laws and antique furniture and glassware from my father. We had more stuff, but we didn't get rid of anything old. Our guest room became a shrine to our formative years: the futon that had been our couch was the guest bed, and our old stereo and TV sat on our former coffee table.

We really needed to start paring down, however; our closets were starting to look a little like my father's house—stacks of boxes that reached from floor to ceiling. But every item had sentimental value, even if I didn't use it. There were blankets and dishes that I'd taken from my dad, and the trinkets that lined my shelves came from all our trips: ceramic fish from Cancun, coconut candles from Hawaii, empty wine bottles from Napa. I liked the souvenirs—sure I had pictures, but I liked the memories these objects evoked.

We requested Germany for Lee's next assignment, and for this move we had to sort everything we owned into three separate shipments: necessities for when we first arrived in the country, a larger shipment that would come a month later, and everything else that we wanted to store for three years. I had to walk through the house asking, "Do I love these garden tools so much that I want to store them for three years? What do I absolutely need when I get there?"

Turns out there are very few things that people truly need. An advisor with the shipping department talked me through the exercise as I laid out the first shipment on the living room floor; it didn't seem like much. She told me to make sure to bring some pots and pans, pillows and lamps, and anything we'd need for work. That was about it.

Helpful friends who had lived in Europe as students warned us to put everything in storage—they claimed the houses were all small there. For overseas moves, though, the military gives people a sponsor who lives in that country, to guide them. Our sponsor told us to bring everything in our house that we wanted to keep. We made some hard decisions, called Goodwill to pick up a truckload of furniture and electronics—all those old pieces we'd kept from our very first place—and got on a plane for Frankfurt.

Living Like Goldilocks

Every home we looked at near Landstuhl, the hospital where Lee would work, was huge and all were constructed with a bizarre use of space. We chose a farmhouse that sat above a little German village. Our landlord explained the strange spatial arrangement: It seems that Germans were taxed on how many rooms made up the square footage of their homes. So rather than a big house with lots of rooms, you'd find a big house with two long rooms divided by outcroppings or shelves or screens. Also, closets counted as rooms so Germans didn't build closets. We had serious storage issues.

The idea of buying more furniture to fill up another house was discouraging. We'd come to Germany to travel; we didn't want to spend money on wardrobes and cabinets that we likely wouldn't need (and couldn't fit) anywhere else. So we improvised, buying cheap storage units and shelves that robbed the charming farmhouse of some of its appeal.

The farmhouse also introduced us to new frustrations. The electricity, the water, the gas, or the phones might go down for days at a time. We'd finally had enough when we came home from a trip to Paris to find everything dark. No electricity. No phones. No hot water. The utility company told us it would be two weeks before we were up and running again.

We moved onto the military base for our last year in Germany, into an apartment that was half the size of the house we'd owned in Texas. We donated boxes of clothes and small appliances, dishes, old flatware, books, and videos, whatever we were willing to part with so that our smaller home could breathe.

I'd gotten used to the privacy of our farmhouse, without neighbors on all sides. No matter how many additional trips I made to the thrift store to offload things and give us more space, the apartment walls were too thin and the neighbors were too close. We'd been traveling every month to see the cities of Europe, but now we found reasons just to get away from the apartment: we'd drive to Luxembourg to try a coffee shop or drive down to France just to get bread.

Then my father died. I flew home to plan his funeral and as I leafed through the prayer cards, the funeral director asked if I'd seen my father's house yet. He told me, "You're in for a shock."

When my dad's antique market changed owners, he had brought all his merchandise home. Of course, there was more to it than that. My parents had divorced and my brother had died a decade earlier. My father had always hoarded, but it had gotten completely out of control. Dusty glass cabinets full of vases and antique trinkets lined the walls, and stacks of magazines clogged the hall. Desks were stacked on top of tables; laundry was piled on the beds and floor and fell out of closets and dresser drawers. In the kitchen, the oven was stuffed with months of mail.

It took me three weeks to clear out my father's house. There was a point when I sat in the rental car down the street from the house and screamed until I lost my voice. The junk went into dumpsters and then I hired an auction house for an estate sale. I kept a chest of photographs and a box of his favorite antique vases. Everything else was sold or trashed. I flew back to Germany feeling bitter and angry and guilty.

A few months later, Lee and I learned that we'd be moving to Hawaii. I was determined that we would move with as few possessions as possible. I now realized that I wanted anything I kept to have real value to me, value I could explain beyond just sentimentalism. Previously,

I couldn't display the hand-painted mask I'd bought during the Venice Carnival because my cabinets were full of plastic cups I'd kept from trips to the county fair. The pen in the velvet box and the hand-written note my dad gave me when I went off to college obviously meant more to me than the promo pens and notebooks that had been littering our kitchen drawers. All these objects didn't have the same value, and yet I had treated them as though they did. When the movers came, they were in and out of our home in less than a day with what we really wanted to keep.

Settling Down for Now

As Lee and I looked for a home in Hawaii, we searched with a better sense of what we needed to live comfortably. We both wanted space and easy access to a town, and I wanted privacy and a nice view if we could get it. We didn't want to buy anything new or give anything away to make our lives fit. We wanted a place where we'd be happy to come home.

In our search, we found two candidates: a spectacular house on a bay with floor-to-ceiling windows, where ocean waves lapped against the shore below, and a pretty house in a beach town that had a glimpse of ocean. The house on the bay was miles from the closest town, and the rent was miles over our budget; the rooms were small, the driveway fed straight into a busy and dangerous highway with a blind spot—but, oh, what a view. We picked the pretty house in town. And even though we had plenty of space, I did another sweep through our boxes as I unpacked, deciding that I didn't have to hold on to every book and T-shirt.

We have one more move left. Hawaii marks the end of Lee's commitment to the military and then we can choose where we want to live, where we want to settle down. After so many moves, I've learned that it doesn't take much to live comfortably. We've pared down and stayed organized, and that opens up the possibilities for the house that will finally be our home.

A MAN ON A MISSION

•

By Fred Ecks

*I*T'S A TUESDAY MORNING IN APRIL. I'M OUT FOR A TRAIL run on a gorgeous day, hoping to finish up before the sun gets too intense. We're having a mild spring, so it's getting rather warm already at ten a.m. As I top Sweeney Ridge in the Golden Gate National Recreation Area on my way to the beach at Pacifica, my mind is drifting off, watching the red-tailed hawks soaring on the drafts.

I remind myself to watch the trail; it's been warm enough recently that it's getting to be the season to keep an eye out for rattlesnakes. I head to the Taco Bell on the beach for a quick brunch of budget tostadas before returning home to our houseboat in South San Francisco.

As I run along, I'm musing about how life has changed for me. Years ago, a Tuesday morning like this would have been an exercise in tiredness, stress, and dissatisfaction. I would sit in my cubicle, trying to wrestle a piece of computer code to do what it's supposed to, so I could finish the task at hand and report the success to my team. I would look outside at the beautiful day, wishing I could be there.

However, there were bills to pay, customers to satisfy, memos and emails to write, and meetings to attend. I didn't have a choice; I needed to keep up with the mortgage and credit card payments. I was only in my late twenties, but I felt like I had strapped myself in for a lifelong ride. I was destined to work full-time in the corporate world for the foreseeable future. I was tired of being tired.

But today, having just turned forty-one, I'm awake. I woke up this morning without an alarm clock, when the sun came up. I got out the door quickly to avoid the midday sun, not because I had a work schedule. I am increasing my mileage on trail runs. With the longer distances, I find myself in spectacular natural places, on hilltops overlooking the ocean and San Francisco Bay. Running farther takes time. Today's will be about a five-hour run. It's a blast, watching the flowers blooming in springtime, the rabbits and deer fleeing my presence, and the surfers riding the waves outside my favorite brunch stop.

Speaking of surfers, I used to wonder how they do that. No, not how they surf—how they live! I mean, it's Tuesday morning. Shouldn't they be at work? Don't they have real jobs? What kind of slackers are they, anyway? In time, I came to figure out a way of life that explains it for me. But first, a little bit of background.

I was born and raised in the Los Angeles area. My parents both worked blue-collar jobs. Dad was a welder. Mom operated a check sorter on the graveyard shift for a local bank branch. They worked full-time to give my brother and me every opportunity in life. We took part in a variety of outdoor activities, including riding bicycles and dirt bikes (motorcycles), playing Little League baseball, and backpacking with the Boy Scouts.

I was interested in putting together model cars and

airplanes, and then moved on to electronic kits. Dad bought me all sorts of kits. I assembled radios, clocks, and even a Heathkit television (Dad and I built that one together). Eventually I gravitated to computers, which is where my career began to develop.

The whole time while my brother and I were growing up, our destinies were clear. We were going to college, getting degrees, and joining the office workforce. That was my personal goal as well, the whole time. With that purpose in mind, I moved quickly and efficiently. I attended an accelerated technical high school, which I completed in three years while receiving a strong practical education in electronic design. I gained admission to Cal Poly in San Luis Obispo, where I began college just before turning eighteen.

My first roommate in the dorms was a guy named John. I didn't understand John. He didn't have a television. I showed up with mine and offered to share it. He appreciated the kind gesture, but he wasn't particularly interested. He was a child development major, which made no sense to me. What sort of job would that degree get him? I was a computer science major, of course. John and I got to be very good friends. Our interests were in different worlds, but we enjoyed each other's company.

In college, I was a man on a mission. I worked hard all the way through, taking just a little time for social interaction. Between an intensive study load and a variety of jobs, I pursued my goal. I graduated with a B.S. degree in computer science right after turning twenty-one. I took my first full-time position as a software engineer in San Diego. To celebrate my success, I bought a brand new motorcycle on credit, and then bought a used Corvette (also on credit) from a used car dealer.

As much as I tried to find happiness in my newfound success, it just wasn't working. I was terribly lonely, missing all of my friends from college. I quickly grew bored with the relatively stagnant day-to-day office life. The toys I bought didn't make me happy. In fact, my beloved Corvette turned out to be a piece of junk. It suffered breakdown after breakdown, and eventually caught fire one day and burned to a crisp. Yes, that was me on the traffic report that morning when the fire trucks had traffic backed up for miles. I replaced the lump of charcoal with a new Honda (again on credit).

After many months of feeling lonely and lost, I decided that it was time to return to the life I preferred. I sold my new car and went back to school for a master's degree. I enjoyed that, but it was fleeting. I quickly completed my advanced degree and was back where I started. I was only twenty-three years old, going back to working full-time as a more-educated software engineer. At least this time I stayed in town with my friends, rather than taking a job far away.

I don't learn fast. I now repeated much of what I had done the first time. I bought another new car, this time a V-8 Mustang. I like toys, so I spent even more to put a supercharger and expensive tires on it. Of course, I still used credit to buy the car. It was the only way I knew.

About this time, I bought my first place, a mobile home in a small trailer park in town. I had a neighbor there who fascinated me. I never got to know him, which was a shame. He didn't own a car. I thought that was the strangest thing! He had some bicycles, and he seemed to have a lot of free time.

One evening in the midst of frustration and boredom with my life of full-time work and car payments, I happened upon an idea. What if I were to trim my life back to the bare necessities? What if I only had my mobile home and some money each month for food, utilities, and health insurance? How much would I have to save to be able to cover all those expenses with just the interest?

I totaled all my base expenses at about $800 a month, or $9,600 a year. Back then, savings interest ran about 8 percent a year, which meant it would take $120,000 saved to pay those expenses with interest alone. With my job, I figured I could save about $1,000 per month. That meant it would take ten years for me to get there. I would be about thirty-four years old, which at the time seemed like an advanced age that I would only reach if I were very, very lucky! It was so far in the future, such an unfathomable goal, that I gave up.

Over the next few years, I found my first love. We married and bought a big house together. But as time went on, I found myself deeper and deeper in the doldrums of dissatisfaction. As I woke up each morning and spent another full day in the office, I longed for the days of college. In college, my life had been vibrant and always new as I worked part-time in a very small company full of fresh and interesting projects, and rapidly learned new concepts with each college class.

But now, having "succeeded" in achieving my professional goals, I desperately needed the space in life to pursue myriad other interests. Two weeks per year of vacation was all I had! I owned six bicycles, a motorcycle, a garage full of power tools, and a whole collection of outdoor equipment. I had a nice big house on a quarter acre with a Great Dane. Alas, I didn't have enough time to enjoy them.

One day I saw a short piece in a local weekly paper discussing current national trends. It said that "frugality" was big, according to the book *Your Money or Your Life*. Thinking back to some of the people I had known who didn't seem to work so much, I bought a copy. As I read it, I was grinning, laughing, and nodding my head as the authors laid out a clear, sure-fire path out of my doldrums that stirred me to action. I wanted my life back!

As we progressed in trimming our expenses, my wife and I paid off our credit cards in a year by making $1000-a-month payments into them. The money came from eating out less, buying fewer new toys, and generally paying more attention to our expenses. With our goal of leaving the full-time rat race behind, we were happy to become frugal.

Eventually, our different levels of dissatisfaction with full-time work came between us. We had different dreams in life. She dreamt of a life that included kids, pets, and a family home. I dreamt of a life of flexibility to pursue travel, outdoor adventures, and lifelong education. We both desperately longed for our individual dreams, so we split up to pursue them. Years later, I see now that we made a good choice. We only would have stifled each other to stay together. Now both of us are happier and more satisfied.

Following my divorce, I moved to Silicon Valley to take a high-income job with a large computer company. Without anyone else to support, I was able to trim my expenses to the bone. I'm no Puritan, though; I used some of the money that would otherwise have been spent on items unimportant to me to afford some extravagances that I really enjoyed. While my colleagues were dropping twenty bucks on lunch each day, I went for the three-buck burrito down the street. I stuck to old used cars and no fancier housing than a downscale rented room with buddies. But then on the weekends, I paid good money to learn how to sail on San Francisco Bay! I kept my expenses low, but not so low that life became drudgery. I kept focused on my big goal of declaring, "ENOUGH!"

After continuing to live this way year after year, I built up a sizable nest egg. I saved fully half of my gross income during that time. I read a lot about investing and carefully invested my money. Once I had a good chunk of savings, I left my corporate job for a nonprofit opportunity in Europe. When I submitted my resignation to my corporate manager, a fantastic guy who had lived abroad, he simply said, "I can't compete with that." As a friend, he recommended I go.

Sure enough, it was a blast. Because I wasn't concerned with making as much money as possible, I was able to immerse myself in the ethical goals of the nonprofit organization. I was living overseas for the first time! I learned the language, culture, and a whole other way of life. In the meantime, I continued to save money from my far-lower nonprofit salary. Because I had become satisfied with a frugal way of life, I had the flexibility to try new experiences that fundamentally changed me. I'll take those experiences over a new car anytime.

After a few more years of saving and investing, I decided to try living without a paycheck. That was over five years ago. During this time, I've discovered that my expenses are even lower when I don't have a job. I cook most of my meals at home now. I don't commute. I take the time to fix things when they break. Simply put, this doesn't take much money.

I'm once again in a long-term relationship. This time, frugality is a shared value. She works half-time for a local nonprofit organization; I live comfortably on interest from my savings. We reside on an old houseboat that we bought for $3,100. Our monthly berth rent is $580 for the two of us. Here in the San Francisco Bay area, that's a very cheap way to live. Our "backyard" has ducks, geese, cormorants, and the occasional seal.

My other basic monthly expenses include groceries, health insurance ($103), electricity, and telephone. Totaling it all up, my basic needs are met for about $600 a month. I spend more than that, but the thing is, it's not stressful for me to pay the bills. Life is easy and simple. Even if my savings were to run short, I wouldn't have to work much to make up for the shortfall.

Sometimes, folks around me who know I'm not working for money seem to think I must be fabulously rich. No, I'm not rich. I'm comfortable. I don't need more. I'm satisfied. What I like to say is, "It's not about how much you have; it's about how little you need."

I used to think that success was a nice house and a new car. I learn slowly, so I had to achieve that goal to figure some things out about myself. Now I know that, for me, success is having the time and flexibility to enjoy life, wherever it takes me.

The Wonderment
of Enough

∎

JUST ENOUGH

•

By Derek Donald Hambrick

I HAVE NO IDEA WHERE I DISCOVERED IT, BUT I KNOW its ripeness of meaning stayed with me. The small clipping, torn from who knows what source, contains a quote from Art Garfunkel. He ponders the word *more*.

> I like that word. "More" is a prayer to God, isn't it? Gratitude and plea, all in one.
> Since I am so appreciative of this life, I want more. I want more family. More time with family. . . .
> So, yes, my future is more, I hope.

What struck me about Art's rumination was the meaning, the beautiful meaning, he found tucked away in that seemingly insignificant, well-used word, *more*. I hadn't thought of the word in such deep terms, preferring to use it between the phrases "Can I have some?" and "Lasagna, please?"

As I thought on it, it seemed that *more* took on another meaning. Yes, gratitude is a part of it, but there's something lacking, a grain of dissatisfaction, perhaps; it's as if *more* says "Thank you, but this isn't enough." That was unsettling.

Because I work with the English language for a living,

I found myself struggling for a better word, a word that would convey that gratitude unreservedly.

What did I find? *Enough.*

Three vowels. Three consonants. A pretty balanced word if you ask me. And appropriate. Appropriate because it applied to what my family was going through when I found Art's wisdom. Given the volitional simplification my family was moving through at the time, I'd consider finding the quote a coincidence if I believed in such things. Instead, I see it as an intricate arrangement.

At that time, I'd been employed with a major airline, enjoyed a modest income with a respectable raise every 365 days, and had adjusted my family's lifestyle accordingly.

It's important to understand that my wife and I have never been extravagant, seeking instead to practice simplicity and show gratitude for our materials and surroundings. Accordingly, we're relatively simple people, happy with what we have. Nonetheless, we had our plans for expanding materially. Bigger house, larger yard, better neighborhood—essentially the same as most other Americans, but determined not to let it get out of control.

Regardless, as I was just cresting the five-year point with my employer, my pay took a sizeable leap. (The extra week of vacation that went along with the increase didn't hurt either.) I suppose it was the two years of living within our means that kept us, as a married couple, from splurging both the money and time off on a trip to some resort. Those kinds of things are *so* much better when you save up for them rather than convoluting your life by putting them on a credit card. Take it from a former travel professional: go abroad nonstop, and don't make a connection through going into debt first.

With a little extra money in the bank and more time to spend with each other, our family was, at least on material and mental levels, more prepared for the future. Enter the events of 9/11. Our republic's ensuing uncertainty seemed to crescendo particularly in the airline industry and still echoes today.

Decreased passenger travel, increased security concerns, and other factors manifested through unfortunate changes for me and countless others in the industry. In retrospect, it was simplicity values that proved their worth in these times of trouble; namely, eliminate all the fluff and stay focused on the basics. At work, that meant focusing on taking care of the customer and providing a safe, enjoyable travel experience. When we focused on that, we couldn't worry. There wasn't space in my consciousness to maintain thoughts of both altruism and anxiety. Funny, I'd say that facet of simplicity applies regardless of one's occupation.

Two significant changes to our lives in the post-9/11 world hit where it counts (or at least where it hurts). Both were pay cuts. The first occurred in December 2001 and measured 10 percent on the Richter scale. The aftershock came a year later, reducing our pay by another 9 percent. Factor in the increased cost of our benefits and, depending on which employee does the play-by-play, the overall drop in compensation weighed in between 22 to 38 percent.

From the perspective of family, the pay cut, as was the

case for everyone, was tremendous. However, given our simple manner of living, we had a sturdy financial position from which we could approach the predicament. It's hard to put into words how grateful we are to have had that advantage. Spiritually, I see our favorable situation as an expression of God's love and protection. Secularly, I see it as ascribing to the concept of simplicity.

I ask myself, *What if* we weren't simple regarding our finances, lifestyle, and so forth? The alternate reality scares me. What if we had gotten a mortgage that was a stretch to pay? What if we had not held on to our cars, paying them off while others had traded them in for larger notes? What if we had fielded any number of balance-carrying credit cards every time we wanted something? The answer is—not unlike the front of my shirt when our three-year-old sneezes with a mouthful of oatmeal—*not a pretty picture.*

Like all of my coworkers and others across varied industries, we were forced to be simple. In our case, we were forced to be simpler than before. Thanks to holding fast to that banner of simplicity, we did more with less and it worked out just fine.

But there's an interesting sprout that broke the surface through all of this: gratitude. The increased simplification, albeit out of necessity, produced more gratitude than what we'd previously felt for our surroundings and circumstances. Like our lighter lifestyle, we've always tried to be grateful, attempting, as exemplified by Kotama Okada, to be "absolutely grateful . . . in every way for all things from morning till night."

A tall order, for sure. Let's just say that the above is a

goal and not a reality in our lives—at the very least in Atlanta traffic. I suppose I'll be divine when my depth of gratitude for finding the perfect parking space matches my depth of gratitude for the grandma in the station wagon who whips around me to grab that space before me.

But check this out: when a person has less, we found it's easier to be grateful for it—less to think about, but more gratitude to allocate to each thing, each experience, and so on. Pretty interesting concept.

What's more, we found that the more we practiced being "simply grateful," the more the things we truly wanted came into our lives.

Take writing for instance. During the tribulation of 2001–02, I came to understand that I wanted to write for a living, so I did. Just about every time I wrote, I was grateful for doing so. Soon, I was able to contribute to an employee publication. Then a monthly employee circular. And then I was asked to be *editor* for the circular. Then I was awarded a position working in employee communications. Today, I'm working with employee communications for another airline at the executive level, a position that has finally brought our income up to a pre-9/11 figure. What's more, I'm meeting with success in writing freelance, not to mention getting published.

Sure it's been a few years in the making, but, in short, I'm doing what I love and it's making the ends meet. Tracing the questions "Why?" or, more appropriately, "How?" we find ourselves surrounded by a divinely created concept: *enough.*

Enough represents a change my family has undergone

and is going through. Not the sensational transformations you hear about like Porsches to public transportation or country clubs to campgrounds, but change on a smaller, yet infinitely more enduring scale. We've taken stock of what we have, counted our blessings as it were, and realized that we have enough. Partially born out of want, partially born out of need, and entirely the better for it, the Hambrick household has simplified.

I feel that we've understood *enough* on a deep level because we were practicing it volitionally before we had to practice it out of necessity. Such is the case with any art or pursuit. You think you get everything out of what you're practicing; you get to the top of the precipice and then . . . then you poke your head over the top just to find another rise that takes you even higher, to an even greater level of expertise, understanding, and appreciation.

Such is the case with simplicity. And the exciting thing is that this is an approach, a philosophy, that you can apply to every experience, in any situation, and toward any kind of . . . well, *stuff* that comes at you.

And believe me when I say it works.

TOOLITTLE, TOOMUCH,
and ENOUGH

•

By Bob Hinschläger

"WHAT DO YOU WANT?"

Now there's a deceivingly uncomplicated question. It seems straightforward enough, but it occurs to me that wants are nothing less than the steering wheel of life. Looking back, I see that I adopted a unique set of desires and expectations for possessions, activities, and social standing, like any other youngster. Although (and maybe because) I was not from a wealthy or materialistic family, my urge was to gather and accumulate. I believed I had Toolittle in life and, short of stealing, if I had the means to get something I thought I could use, I latched on to it. I was driven by my wants.

I smile now, thinking of my parents' struggle to keep a lid on my collecting urge. To their annoyance, there was a landfill next to the road I walked to and from school. Not a garbage dump, this was more a pond-filling project where old sidewalk slabs, paving bricks, and dump truckloads of other solids were interspersed with real treasures—maybe a broken toolbox, an old office chair, or other such jetsam. After school, we boys would scurry down the crumbly dirt bank, stepping carefully through the continuously replenished supply of stuff, in search of underrated finds. Then, along with my gym bag and books, I'd tote home any castoffs I believed were too good to throw away.

To my parents' way of thinking, I started trying to stockpile Toomuch way too early and, typically, they sent me hoofing back to the pond after supper to redeposit the treasures. In those early days, my parents' wisdom served to regulate my collecting. Later, while I served in the navy, Uncle Sam kept an absolute lid on my propensity to accumulate anything more than bare essentials with a tiny shipboard locker. Later still, with a place of my own and the freedom to overindulge, I developed the ability to navigate that slippery slope between Toolittle and Toomuch as follows. Bit by bit, I found Enough.

Toolittle

As a husband and father, I now understand Toolittle as a shortfall in basic health, responsibility, or fulfillment. For example, if medical care, nutrition, shelter, sanitation, or healthful activity were in short supply, my family's health would suffer. That would be Toolittle. If I were unable to provide security for my wife or clothing, learning opportunities, and nurturing experiences for my children, that too would qualify as Toolittle. Also, because such things as music, worship, engaging pastimes, and community service are helpful and healthful, Toolittle could result here as well.

For example, when I took on the responsibilities of a new home owner, I found myself hampered everywhere I turned by my lack of tools. For me, that qualified as

Toolittle. Exploring estate auctions, mastering garage sales, and poking through secondhand stores, I entertained myself with the hunt for low-cost, high-quality yard and household tools, buying all I needed. This exercise in thriftiness paid off, eventually building up momentum that could have rolled right over me. It may sound silly, but for me, the double lure of good stuff that's cheap is intoxicating.

After a few years of remarkable bargains and gathering a tool arsenal that rivaled my dad's lifetime accumulation, I had to resist that third leaf rake for just a buck. I needed to recognize that one claw hammer in the shop and another in the house is Enough. Although it hadn't hurt me yet, I had passed through Toolittle and stood at the threshold of Toomuch, where excess good stuff could eventually strangle me.

Toomuch

Thanksgiving Day dinner is always a time when, how should I say this, I eat too much. I heard somewhere that it takes twenty minutes for the stomach's "full" message to get to the brain. Too often though, I spend those twenty minutes blissfully piling and devouring more delicious stuff. Without control, even a good thing (like Mom's pecan pie), long anticipated and perfect in its presentation, can ultimately make me miserable.

Although sometimes difficult to explain, that's how it is for me with Toomuch. I usually recognize or admit I have reached Toomuch only after feeling the painful effects. Stealthily, Toomuch tends to pile up in the backwater, the low-energy places where it's allowed to rest. Like dust bunnies in a corner, it accumulates until it is eliminated, so I don't want it to even get a toehold in my life.

Like many others, however, I recognize my inclination toward accumulating Toomuch and don't really feel shame in that. I am blessed to live in a country where market forces, representative democracy, and hard work have resulted in personal prosperity. It is only natural to benefit from that. At the same time, I recognize that personal abundance requires management and constraint if it is to remain the servant and not a master, with costly demands in dollars, time, space, and lost opportunities.

For instance, when I see those weekend sale ads scream "Save," I almost get sucked in before realizing the real message is "Spend." Car and furniture stores aren't urging me to save. They want me to bring them my money. Deep down I know that $100 off any price is no bargain if the object contributes to Toomuch. I am better off truly saving the "unbelievably low price" by not paying it at all.

While raising two talented daughters, I also had to help regulate our cumulative family obligations to prevent Toomuch in the area of activities. Just a couple of years separated my daughters' ages, and school plays, choir, the church youth group, piano lessons, band activities, and 4H all beckoned for their attention—and all offered valuable benefits. There's an old saying, "Be careful what you wish for because you might get it." Beyond their required schoolwork, these girls simply had so many excellent options that Dad had to help prioritize and limit activities to prevent family activity from becoming Toomuch.

Space problems can be another cost of Toomuch. We have shared kitchen table space with bills, magazines, and trinkets between and even during meals. While this is not completely under control in our kitchen yet, I do draw the line and simply refuse to allow Toomuch to accumulate in closets and the garage. Otherwise, I would be paying real estate taxes to keep a roof over Toomuch while my car deteriorated outdoors. Here in Ohio, that means scraping snow and ice too—yet another cost.

Finally, the overarching cost category for me is lost opportunity. If I accumulated Toomuch, I would wonder what else could have been done with that money. With that time. With that resource. I believe that the pursuit of Toomuch is far too common when a survey paid for by Hilton Hotels finds that "as a culture we place a higher value on our success in the workplace than our success at home." That isn't the focus I want. I want that narrow, sweet spot of Enough veiled between Toolittle and Toomuch.

Enough

Having survived fifty-plus years of life so far, I have dozens of reminiscences to fascinate my grandchildren. But one of my favorite memories in life is of a single evening invested with a good friend as we chatted and passively observed his pasture. As the two of us lolled in worn lawn chairs in the dark sweat of a humid August night, we enjoyed a few icy brews and appreciated our similarly blessed, simple lives.

Idly watching the full, yellow moon arc across the

eastern sky to spookily illuminate a pair of lazing cattle, John recounted how he'd received them from a neighbor in a trade for the hay in his idle pasture. John was satisfied with the swap even though they both knew the hay was worth more than the two steers. As the curious beasts roamed near again to watch us watching them, John justified his contentment: each man received a good deal. John acquired two unhurried, grass-fed beef cattle, free to graze and water and sleep at will throughout the summer. Come winter, there would be a freezer full of outstanding steaks, roasts, and burgers to last another year.

Enough, obviously, means something different to everyone. To my friend John, Enough meant he didn't have to negotiate top dollar for his rich stand of alfalfa mix hay and he didn't have to speculate on whether he could have done better. It meant two cattle would provide his family (and a good number of friends) with wholesome, clean meat for the coming year so there was no need for more. For both John and me, Enough meant that a long evening spent numbering our blessings by a hazy, moonlit cow pasture was memorable entertainment.

The pure concept of Enough in my own life is difficult for me to isolate. Contentment between "wanting to get" and "wanting to get rid of" is inextricably entwined with thrift, generosity, and a recognition that God's natural systems are made to work together. I'm not sure anymore where one ends and the others intersect, but I am sure that embracing Enough is not an exercise in doing without. It's a part of living better. Rather than pursuing happiness through attaining "the dream," my concept of

Enough has developed from taking a good look at my dream—that is, what I really want.

Consider, for a moment, my vegetable garden where the perennial vision is wholesome work and natural ingredients combining through nature to produce complete, healthful foods for our family and friends. Toward that end, year-round we compost vegetable scraps because a handful of rich compost gets each springtime seedling off to a vigorous start. I trade a few jars of home-canned pickles to borrow a rototiller for the necessary three hours each year to prepare the ground. And when the soil warms, I heavily mulch with leaves or goat barn straw to stop weeds (and weeding!) until it's all turned under to enrich next year's soil.

Obviously, gardening is not for everyone and this is not the easiest way to garden. Commercial fertilizers, for instance, are easy to use and may grow bigger veggies, but my method arguably produces better-tasting and more nutritious food, provides exercise, and builds up soil for sustained productivity. Additionally, garden chores and running compost outdoors are good chances for young ones to help the family and learn responsibility too. My gardening method provides many of my "dream" benefits while avoiding the cost and drawbacks of fertilizers. For me, it is Enough.

For another example, is there more excess anywhere today than in kids' toys; that enormous variety of playthings, most with instructions for parents? Truthfully, my children's greatest fun always came from play they invented. From the recycling bag came paper towel rolls, oatmeal boxes, and cardboard that they converted into toys and even a lap desk with pencil holder. Similarly, a tarp and rope have variously served as a tent, a hammock, a swimming pool, and who knows what else.

While making use of common materials, the kids learned youthful physics lessons, developed motor skills, exercised their imaginations, and practiced social skills—all while having fun! I never saw a reason to load them up with seldom-used, structured-play games and toys. Here too, Enough wasn't poverty to be survived. Fewer "play this way" toys, I believe, actually enhanced life for our next generation.

Here's the nutshell. I can picture myself dragging suitcases and overstuffed bags through a bustling airport while trying to keep tickets, a drippy hot dog, a cup of hot coffee, and a small child under control. Encumbered with so many belongings, I could easily miss my flight, or that precious child could become just another burden. I have come to recognize that too much stuff weighs me down and makes the going harder and less enjoyable than it ought to be. Consequently, my practice now is to order my life to achieve what I truly believe is important. I manage my wants and pack lightly for the trip.

TRADING CALIFORNIA
FOR KENTUCKY

•

By Teena Hammond Gomez

THIS MORNING, I WAS OUTSIDE ADMIRING THE COUN-
try view from my five-acre parcel in the rolling hills of
Kentucky. It was a quiet moment with only the sound of
the geese overhead and the occasional cow bellowing at a
newly born calf. It's a scene that I enjoy daily as I weed
my garden and learn new ways of organically keeping
those pesky beetles off the emerging potato vines.

It's quite a different experience from my life exactly
one year ago, when I lived in southern California on a
relatively tiny lot with barely any room for a garden. At
one point, I was commuting four hours daily to my job as
a magazine writer in Santa Monica.

In California, I worked at various publications, including *People* magazine, interviewing celebrities and report-
ing on what was hot and what was not. I spent my time
at black-tie affairs and award shows such as the Academy
Awards and the Golden Globes. Lunch at The Ivy, a famous Los Angeles eatery, was commonplace. Scoring
that all-important one p.m. lunch reservation at The
Grill in Beverly Hills was essential. I never parked my
own car. It was always valet, even at the doctor's office. If

I wanted to go shopping, I went to the hot spots in town on Robertson Avenue and Third Street.

My husband, Joe, who is an information technology manager, had an equally long commute. He worked in Manhattan Beach and would leave home before sunrise, returning after dark. We were always exhausted and too tired to enjoy each other's company or even cook dinner together. It was not a satisfying way of life.

Despite my husband being a California native with family nearby, he was ready to move out of the state. We knew we had to do something to simplify and enhance the quality of our lives.

Since I am a Kentucky native, it seemed natural to move back to my home state. During a holiday trip home in December 2005, my husband and I spent time touring every available parcel of land between five and ten acres in a tri-county area. We were determined to find that perfect spot to build our dream home. After three days of searching, there were three properties left that we hadn't seen. It was nearing sunset on the day before Christmas Eve and we knew we had to choose a property soon, or wait until our next trip in the summer. My mother, a real estate agent, said we could probably just make it to one more location before dark and we should pick one from the three. I had enjoyed a good feeling about one particular spot all day long and had been dying to see it. I knew that the real estate listing could be deceptive, as had many that day. But this one in particular really spoke to me.

So we turned the car around and headed to the historic town of Shelbyville, Kentucky, population 10,700. We drove a few miles south of the main downtown area and pulled onto a charming, peaceful country road dotted with 1800s-era mansions and horse farms. My excitement grew as we turned onto the road that would become our future. I knew that we'd found it, our dream spot. On that cold December day at dusk, as my husband and I stood on the windy hill overlooking a hundred-acre valley below, we hugged and smiled as we knew we'd found paradise. We immediately dubbed it "The Golden Farm" in honor of our three golden retrievers.

We closed on the property the next month and, at that point, figured it would take about a year until my husband found the perfect job to allow us to make the big move. But fate intervened and my husband landed an ideal job very quickly. With all relocation expenses paid, how could we say no? We sold our California home and moved to Kentucky in the summer of 2006, with our dogs and twelve-year-old tabby cat in tow.

The ironic part was that our friends in California understood why we wanted to move to simplify our lives. But our friends in Kentucky couldn't figure out why we'd even consider leaving such a beautiful state as California, which had what they perceived to be perfect weather. But, of course, the advantages are apparent to those who have spent two hours in traffic to drive fifteen miles versus those who haven't. And to those who have had to stay indoors on polluted days when the air quality is poor. And to those who have heard the police helicopters circling their home overhead as they search for criminals.

So we moved to Kentucky and immediately began construction on our new home and, of course, a barn. We finally moved into our house in April 2007, and our first purchase was a new John Deere tractor. My garden was plowed at the same time as our new life began. We planted an orchard with sixteen different types of fruit trees, ten blueberry bushes, thornless blackberries, and a strawberry patch. My mom teased that I'd need to put in a drive-through window in order to feed my husband, since he never seemed to get off his tractor.

Another irony came last fall, during the muddiest part of our construction. I had ruined several pairs of shoes and needed a new pair that would hold up to all the mud and rain. I found myself debating on which pair of muck boots to buy at a tractor supply store. On the drive home, I started laughing as I realized that the year before I was buying my shoes on Rodeo Drive and now I was buying them at a farm store. I loved the contrast between the two different lifestyles.

The best part is, we didn't have to downsize our life to simplify it and add satisfaction. We live on five beautiful acres on one of the highest points in the county. We built a 3,600-square-foot country house with a 2,400-square-foot walk-out basement—nearly twice the space of our previous home in California. The difference is now we don't have neighbors twenty feet from our house. When I lived in densely populated Hermosa Beach before I married, my neighbors used to complain that my dining room lights were keeping them up at night because the lights illuminated their bedroom. The buildings were that close together.

Now there are only three houses even in view of our own. And our neighbors are so nice and welcoming. We purposely put large covered front and back porches on our house so that we could sit and wave at the neighbors as they pass. Our rural street is so quiet that it could be an hour before someone drives by.

The healthy lifestyle in the country has made life a joy. My husband and I are relative newlyweds, having married in August 2003. We'd spent our lives working on our careers, so finding each other, marrying at age thirty-five, and soon after creating our dream home is an amazing experience. We feel so fortunate to be able to live in a wonderful home on a beautiful piece of land.

Instead of commuting four hours to and from an office, I now work from home as a freelance writer. Instead of a view of Wilshire Boulevard, I now look out onto a hundred-acre valley filled with cows, wild turkeys, and geese, as my dogs sleep at my feet and my cat curls up on my desktop. It's an experience I wouldn't trade for anything.

My husband, who spent ten years commuting three to four hours roundtrip to work daily, now works just nine miles down the road. It's so nice to have him nearby and to know that he's safer without spending all of that time in crazy Los Angeles traffic. And when he gets home, he always heads out to his barn to jump on his tractor and work on our property while I make dinner in my custom-designed kitchen. (As I mentioned, simplifying doesn't mean downsizing—I have fabulous appliances and a beautiful kitchen!)

In the short time we've lived in our new home, we've both already lost weight by exercising more as we walk around the property, gardening, and doing other work. Plus, we sleep more soundly at night and my lifelong migraine headaches have mysteriously ended. Our dogs are even healthier, having slimmed down as they run around the five acres, chasing imaginary creatures and tracking down interesting scents.

And then there is the sense of community here in our small town. Nothing like it existed for us in California. When I go into the drugstore, I run into the wonderful woman who grooms my dogs. When I visit the grocery store, I see the contractor we hired to build our barn. And everyone waves at each other when passing in a car.

Even the coffeehouse in town is a treat. Instead of getting a latte fix at Starbucks, I go to my locally owned coffee spot that roasts its own beans. The coffeehouse is part of the tapestry of the community, with book clubs meeting there monthly and book signings for local authors.

My husband has made great friends with our neighbors. One neighbor stopped by just the other day to drop off packets of seeds for our garden. He said it's an annual routine—he buys seeds by the pound and then shares them with his neighbors. When my husband purchased his new tractor, another neighbor pulled us over on the side of the road one day as we passed to let my husband know that, in these parts, when a man gets a new tractor, he drives it down to show the neighbors. Our neighbor laughed and said he couldn't wait to check it out up close. The next morning, I looked out the window to see my husband happily driving away in his tractor as he went to visit the neighbors.

But for now, it's time to work on my garden again. The forecast is promising rain so it's the perfect time to plant those extra rows of corn and beans, so I can harvest them throughout the summer. I look forward to my vegetables and melons ripening not only so that we can enjoy them, but so that I can hand them out to my kind neighbors. It's a special feeling to live in a real community at long last, to have enough. And it's wonderful to know that you can, indeed, go home again.

A KEY TO ENOUGH

•

By Ruth Pittard

M Y KEY RING HAS TWO KEYS ON IT NOW, NOT THE NINE
it held less than two years ago, but still one more than
the single key to which I aspire. I have come to judge the
complexity of my life by the number of keys on my ring,
itself a single round circle with no grocery code readers,
no symbols, and no ID card entry attached. One of the
two remaining keys opens the office door where I volunteer three days a week; the second opens the front door
to a tiny furnished house I am renting on Whidbey
Island, Washington. Nine keys reduced to a duo represents a long journey, but one that has been eminently satisfying and life enhancing at every turn, even with
surprises and challenges. The departed keys have opened
more and more of my time and my life; each relinquished
key has unlocked pieces of my soul.

How did I get here, a woman of fewer and fewer keys
in a world that measures success by larger and larger
numbers? I listened to my inner voice, I questioned some
"key" assumptions, and I opened myself to my own creativity and possibilities.

In my fifty-ninth year, at the height of my earning
power and my career—working a tremendously satisfying but exhausting sixty-hour-a-week job as a college

assistant dean for community service—I woke one spring morning at the usual 5:30 a.m. with questions screaming loudly in my head. Is owning and maintaining a house alone worth having no free time or money? Is my career in community service worth having no time to reflect on what a community is, how it behaves, or how I fit into it? Is being available to work 24/7 worth sacrificing time with my own children and grandchildren, and with myself?

In this most satisfying age so far, when I have accumulated experience and wisdom, love and patience, do I want to spend my time inside an institution, no matter how exciting and fulfilling it is? The answers came quickly and emphatically: "No. No. No. No." I want to make a life more than I want to make a living.

Naturally, the next thought was a large, "But . . ." followed by another set of equally compelling questions. What about my personal and financial security? What about building money for retirement? Where will I live? What will I do? How will I pay my bills? And the question my mother asks me, even though I am sixty: What about health insurance? The first set of questions held sway, however, so less than a month later, the solid asset of my house turned into a liquid one (it sold in less than a week without advertising!). Taking a year to extricate myself from my work, I scheduled the year after that to figure out what the next segment of my life would look like.

In less than six months, I had given away or sold most of my belongings. In less than a year from that fateful wake-up morning, I was living in a friend's loft with still too many books, my grandmother's corner cupboard, a large wardrobe, a chest of drawers from my other grandmother's side of the family, a couple of paintings, my quilts, a new computer, and about a fourth of my wardrobe. I felt light, uncomplicated, and happy. The questions now were, What is the purpose of my life? How can I personify and live what I believe most effectively? What feeds my spirit? How will my life enhance the world?

Loud voices had told me all my life that acquiring more and better grades, clothes, jewelry, money, property, cars, positions, and countless other things would feel good, would make me successful. Initially, all that acquisition did give me some pleasure, but I always felt out of balance, like something just didn't nurture me in that system and I was missing an obvious key concept for my life. Especially during my job in community service, my life felt rich compared to the people with whom I was working, yet by world standards I was not rich. Where did I want to fall on that continuum of money? I would now have time to ask and answer that question and several more, because I had bought time to think.

For the first time since beginning to work at fifteen, my life contained space for reflection, space for rest, and space for spiritual questioning and learning. What is enough for this next part of my life? What is a want and what is a need? How does what I acquire affect the earth? How am I connected to everything around me?

Years ago my son taught me a valuable lesson. "Mom," he said, "there are two ways to be rich. One is to make a lot of money and the other is to modify your needs." This year I read a quotation from Thoreau that echoes his words: "I make myself rich by making my wants few." In this year of living on a very fixed and very limited budget, wants have almost disappeared and needs have shrunk dramatically. Inquiry around purchase guides my intentional choices. Need and want live identified in ways that guide my days.

However, the one need and want I value the most now, in my new life, is my friends, who during and after my year of divestment housed me, encouraged me, loved me, and fed me. Doing more, having more, buying more did not build my heart; living with and investing in friends did. They will be with me always; they and their generosity travel with me, paradoxically occupying little space, but filling my life to overflowing. And in my freedom from daily routine, new friends appear regularly, all with generous hearts and ready to trade the things I don't have for whatever I can give to them. It's a beautiful system; it's a system that nourishes and satisfies. It's a system that feels right for me in this time. It fits my life and purpose.

Most people hearing my story react dramatically to what they perceive as a precarious position in relation to retirement. They worry about catastrophically expensive disease and lack of financial security in my older age. Many express concern that I will be dependent on friends and/or family to take care of me. All are legitimate concerns. All assume that money, a job, and material goods provide security. I, however, assume that love and service make a secure life and, since both produce actions, I am compounding love and service while growing the interest daily. I feel more secure than I ever did making house payments, car payments, tax payments, and lawn-care payments. I intend to give until it is my turn to receive.

So . . . what have I learned on my journey to enough?

Since I have sold my house, I have decided that I will use houses already built, that I will not expend my resources to own land, and that I will think in the smallest terms possible about my remaining years of habitation. Three hundred square feet feel comfortable and spacious, and they will hold whatever I need and want. In addition, I need a closet, access to water, some electricity, light, good textures and colors, a space to sit and lie down, cleanliness, and order. This small space is enough; I've tested it and I know.

I love my ones-of-things: the single beautiful picture; the one antique vase from my grandmother, holding flowers from the roadside; the favorite blue lamp with gold tassels; and the table that holds food, then computer, then folded laundry. Everything has a use, then another one. Everything serves a purpose. Everything suits me. A few aesthetically pleasing and extremely functional belongings suffice for me.

Enough money means money that will sustain my needs for transportation, food, shelter, thrift store purchases, health insurance and doctors, medicine, dentist visits, movies, and the occasional splurge on cloth, jewelry, or music. On Whidbey Island, without a car, I have found rides that have led to friendships. Living simply opens access to so much community lived around pooling resources, riding together, eating together, and occupying mutual spaces. Thrift stores have everything I need, all gently used with plenty of life left in whatever I buy. New is definitely overrated. Owning a car, since I have bought time, seems superfluous where there are friends and buses. Or at least I should share one.

Enough time looks like spending one whole afternoon in a hammock watching a large, elegant garden spider spin its web and construct an egg sack. Never again will spiders appear expendable. Never again will I purposely destroy a web. Now spiders jump into my consciousness everywhere. They are precious works of nature, artists extraordinaire.

And what a luxury to be able to think a thought through, to experience the world in discreet pieces, to read uninterrupted, to completely finish a conversation, to act intentionally with forethought, to walk and appreciate the landscape in clumps rather than bits. To listen and listen and listen more deeply still. To create, discard, and create again, better the second time. To appreciate slowness, cooking from scratch, and time to hear wind and rain.

Being able to see most of what I own in two glances, having one set of clothes on my body and one in the wash, walking with a stick, and meeting kind and generous people everywhere all keep a smile on my face. Practicing personal peace in each daily moment, as a model for world peace, fills my days. Though society might consider me "poor," I have enough of everything that I know is important: family, friends, laughter, health, joy, nature, time, gratitude. I do not pine for anything I've given away or for any future desire. If someone gave me a million dollars tomorrow, I would continue my life with few changes and would work to enhance the world with the money.

I'm still learning how to maximize everything I spend, how to consume less, and how to remember that I live to put *being* as well as *doing* at the spiritual foundation of my life. I believe that our hearts grow in direct proportion to the time we spend cultivating and feeding them. Now that my energy isn't centered on what I own, I can expend it daily on service to others, on reading, on growing my connection to earth, people, and my own soul. In fact, I'm headed toward discarding another key. Which one will it be? And better yet, how would no keys feel?

Cruising to
Satisfaction

■

SMALL MOMENTS

•

by Beth Herndon

SITTING IN A ROOM ON A COLD WINTER DAY, WITH A fire crackling and something warm to drink, I would say that I have found the satisfaction of enough in quiet moments. Moments that in the grand scheme of things seem so small you could pass by them and think them unimportant. You could snap a finger or blink an eye and they would be gone. But they are the kind of twinklings that have changed my life. They are interwoven into the fabric of each new day.

I am a night-shift nurse at a large hospital in the Southeast. I have met many patients whose life stories have inspired me. I talk with them while giving out medications, answering questions, and carrying out nursing procedures. I always hope each night when I work with my patients that I will get a glimpse into who they are. One such glimpse of a patient I will not soon forget is Ben. I met him—and encountered joy—a few months ago.

Ben is a three-year-old boy. He has the most beautiful eyes I have seen in a child. Big, rich, and brown, his eyes are framed by long, curling eyelashes. But what shines most from this little person is his happiness. His infectious smile and rambunctious giggles seem to mark everything he does and says. Some people have a gift of smiling more easily and naturally than the rest of us. He is one of them.

When I first met him, Ben had a white turban made out of medical dressings wrapped around his head. In his three short years, Ben has been suffering multiple seizures, which is why he came to stay with us at the hospital. I learned so much from the nights I spent as his nurse.

On one particular night, we kept having difficulties with Ben's IV, and within the span of twenty-four hours, he required two new IV lines started on his little arm. This meant needles and three people holding him down and big, elephant tears. Because we were often having trouble with these IV lines, I would have to take hold of his arm where an IV was and work with it. Each time I drew near to Ben's arm, he would shrink back in fear and start whimpering, "No, no, no." Those are the kind of moments when I hate my job. Nurses never get used to doing things that hurt children. But then, a few minutes later, the smiles would come again and his giggles would fill the air.

I sat at the nurse's station often during my shifts with Ben those nights, as one of my tasks was to watch the seizure patients' video monitors located there at the desk. Ben's room was right across from the station, and when his door was open, we were within a few feet of each other. He could spy on me from his bed. Several times throughout the evenings, when I would turn in my chair to check on him, he would meet my eyes, clasp his hands together, laugh, and then blow me a kiss. Pure, free love.

Kids are so good at giving it. Joy is as much a part of Ben's makeup as are his hair and eye color.

It is moments like the ones I had with Ben when the big, loud aspects of my life become silenced, if I will let them, and I am left to think about what that person or that instant is trying to tell me. Children constantly remind me of the beauty of simplicity and of capturing what is really most important every day. Watch them dissect a dandelion, or dance and twirl across a parking lot, and you can get lost in their wonder. It is right there in the middle of those times when I know that I have found more than enough for what I need in the midst of the bigger, uncertain, and challenging parts of my life. They are often what urge me on.

Besides being a nurse, I am also a nature lover and avid outdoor adventure seeker. When the grind and demands of work begin to feel like too much, I am learning that time outside is what I need. I often crave the stillness and quiet of the woods.

Several months ago I experienced an especially challenging few weeks at work. Fall was upon us, so that meant the beautiful leaves that change colors to usher in the autumn were abounding. And I was working nights, which meant I was sleeping the loveliest season in Tennessee away. Those days always feel fresh and crisp; they bring bonfires and toasty warm drinks to my mind.

I was driving to the hospital on one of those fall nights when I received a telephone call from my friend Heather. She invited me on a canoe trip the following week. Everything inside me felt like it might burst with the invitation. I needed it in more ways than I realized.

"You're going canoeing?! Today?" my dad had asked when I talked to him the next week. I was about to leave for the trip that day, and nothing could have deterred me, not even the cold. This particular day was gray and unusually frigid for that time of year. But my days at work were leaving me feeling burned out, downtrodden, and very gray myself.

So I joined my friends early in the morning at our meeting point, and we drove to the river. After arriving there we put our boats in and set off together down the icy cold waters. There were mountains around us, clearing gray skies with hints of blue, and dear company. Cindy, Heather, Alex, and Josh were my companions for the day.

Cindy has a quiet confidence and does not need words to fill a space. Heather breathes South African loveliness. Alex is full of life, bringing fun and humor to any situation, but has a strong serious side that makes for an altogether neat person. And Josh is a man who was meant for another time. He lives in ways that are unorthodox for our modern technological age, always wearing a smile, holding peace in his heart, and bringing a lightness to situations.

As I settled into my canoe and began to paddle down the river, I realized how amazing it felt to use my muscles in a productive way, all the while taking in the sights and sounds around me. Birds chirped, singing their songs to one another; hawks flew overhead; fish jumped in and out of the water. The lush green and undulating hills of Tennessee brought satisfaction to my mind after days of machines, walls, and sickness. It was as if the weary places in me fell off with each stroke forward and something else moved into their place inside of me. I was slowly being renewed and refreshed.

We spent the day exploring the river and countryside, laughing and being quiet together. After our canoe ride was finished, we loaded up the cars to head for a campsite for the night. We stopped at a quaint country home on our way, after seeing a sign with fresh apple cider for sale posted at its driveway's edge. On the driveway to the home, we were met by a cheerful older gentleman and his grandson, who later sent us away with a gallon of homemade cider and fresh jam.

That evening found us by the campfire, sharing good conversation under a sky full of stars. A lake was several feet in front of us and, as the waters gently lapped in, once again I felt the heaviness in me depart and peace rush in.

The next morning I took a solitary walk by the shore and was full of gratitude for the rescue of the outdoors. I felt as though a weight had been lifted from my shoulders. I am most at home in nature and in the fellowship of warm hearts and good conversation. I savor a good meal and homemade snacks. For those few days, in the middle of all my favorite things, I learned these moments must be purposefully cultivated in my life.

I left that day feeling recharged and ready to begin the workforce grind again. My body felt better, my mind was more at ease, and my spirit was at rest. It was a good moment that was larger than all the trying ones of the previous days. A beautiful moment is like that.

Another smaller moment happened just the other day.

I was sitting in a living room with a group of college friends, including Seth and Carrie. A little over a year earlier, a phone call from Carrie had quickly led to sobs and sadness. She had just suffered a miscarriage and was feeling the deep pain of loss. Sitting there listening to her, and crying with her on the phone, I had realized that somehow in the passage of time we had become adults who were suddenly dealing with very adult things, and none of us knew quite how to do it.

But fast-forward to the other day in that living room, and I see Carrie, glowing happily and talking baby talk to her new son, Colt, whom she is holding on her lap. I see Seth beside her, grasping his new son's hand (Colt is raising his eyes and cooing), and then I realize that only a baby could bring out such joy in him. I look at the faces of the rest of our college friends and see their excitement over this new arrival as well.

Even though we are still learning this thing called adulthood, we are holding tight to one another and, as Seth was, to the new little hands of hope. And we are making our way. I loved that moment. It was full of re-birth, a circle of love, safety, and contentment. I will forever be grateful for the simple truth I learned in that moment: through time, love, healing, and one another mourning really can be turned to dancing.

There are a million more moments like these when I have found the satisfaction of enough. I also find it in simple things like the smells of my mother's Southern home cooking, in a really good haircut, or in a painting that expresses something I have long felt but could not put into words. Then there's an older couple bickering in the midst of a long-enduring relationship, who eventually grasp hands in both utter defeat and triumph simultaneously. At the end of life and the end of the day, what really matters is having someone you love close by, not whether or not you are actually right. It is sitting by the ocean and seeing the waves roll in, taking in a beautiful sunset, or watching a fierce storm.

And everyone has their own favorite songs and musical artists who speak to the truest places of who they are. I tend toward the bluesy, slow, earthy stuff. So whether I am driving to work, cleaning the house, or washing the car, I can pop some tunes in and feel instantly lighter; where I am is okay.

These are the little things that enable me to feel I have enough in a world that often leaves me wanting for more. So as I age and continue on my journey, I am learning to ask not so much the bigger, weightier questions of my life, but of my heart instead. "What are your truest desires?"

And as my heart answers back, often quietly but deeply, I am learning to make time for those desires. I am learning that I cannot make it without them. In some cases, it is a person. Sometimes, it is a place. It could be a smell or a visual or a tactile feeling. But whatever it is, afterward I am never left wanting. Instead, I feel full—I have more than enough.

THE ECONOMICS OF TIME

•

by Erik Richardson

HE APPROACH TO A LIFE OF HAPPINESS THROUGH SIMPLIC-
ity is often portrayed as the result of a movement counter
to the trends and reasoning of the modern, profit-driven
society. For many of us, then, the possibility of exploring
such a lifestyle has seemed risky. I always felt as though I
was being asked to give up a mode of thinking that I have
depended on my whole life. As it turns out, in the course
of some work I was doing on corporate environmental
ethics, I started to realize that this whole way of framing
the options builds upon a mistake in reasoning. Instead of
setting aside the traditional mindset that told me my
goals should be to maximize profit and live a life driven
by value calculations and cost-benefit analyses, I found
that these tools were exactly what I needed to map out a
life of simplicity and satisfaction.

As a good introduction to what this means for my
lifestyle, you can look no further than the beat-up old car
I drive. I learned in graduate school that a car, like a lot
of things, is a depreciating asset, no matter how fancy. In
and of itself, that may not seem to be a shocking revelation. To me, it was a splash of cold water. Let's see how
that ends up affecting my profits and my happiness.

During the years after graduating from my M.B.A. program here in the cold north central region, I came to realize that my body is also a depreciating asset. There is nothing like shoveling thirteen inches of wet snow off the driveway to point out that my back just doesn't work quite like it used to when it was newer. In fact, as I seem to forget more and more things with each birthday, I am beginning to suspect that my brain is also a depreciating asset. That one is not as clear, because I have trouble re-membering whether it used to work better or not.

So, to review, there are now three depreciating assets at work in my story—a car, a body, and (maybe) a mind. Actually there are more, but for now let's keep it at three. If my wife sees a list of how many things around here are breaking down, she's going to make me turn off the com-puter and fix something. Into this mixture, now, we will add an economic concept called opportunity cost.

Opportunity cost is a simple enough idea, though overlooked on a surprisingly large scale. The basic prin-ciple is that whenever we spend money on one thing, we pass up the opportunity to spend it on something else. If the government spends its money on bombers, for in-stance, it passes up the opportunity to spend it on educa-tion. If I decide to buy a new flat-screen television, I can no longer spend that money on a better car stereo sys-tem. This works the same way for both money and time. If I spend time working at the office to pay for my new car, I pass up using that time to, say, go for a hike or head over to the gym for a workout. (Of course, there are far more Sirens of Stuff calling me toward the reefs than just a car or a flat-screen television!) For now, let's just have the car stand in for any of those shiny, fancy goodies of the material marketplace that I sometimes think I might want or need in order to be happy.

Knowing that things have an opportunity cost, though, doesn't get me very far by itself. In order to make this useful, I have to weigh those alternatives against each other. (This is something we're all familiar with, even if we don't think of it in these terms.) This is where we really start to see the tools of economic reasoning come into play—three tools in particular: scarcity, diminishing marginal utility, and investment versus consumption.

Actually, the first two are closely related aspects of the idea of supply and demand, but for this story it helps to talk about them separately. The former, scarcity, just points to the fact that as something gets more and more rare, the value tends to increase. The latter, diminishing marginal utility, points out that as we get more and more of something, we tend to enjoy each addition less and less. If, like me, you've ever gone back for that third helping of pumpkin pie during the holidays, you can probably appreciate this on a pretty concrete level.

Aside from helping me resist that third piece of pumpkin pie from time to time, though, these ideas also keep me on the track toward a simpler life in general. Imagine it's Saturday afternoon. I could put in a couple hours of work on a client project at the office, or I could wander off to the nearby college campus with my nine-year-old daughter to fly kites. Temptingly, if I do a great job on the client project, there's a small bonus in it for me. The thing is, though, I already make a decent enough salary.

Increasing my salary by a tiny bit more has a pretty small impact on my happiness (because of that diminishing utility thing I mentioned). In contrast, how many kite-flying days do you ever really get with your kids? It's valuable because it is scarce for many people. So those thousands of dollars I spent on my education have allowed me to calculate that I should clearly take the afternoon off from client work and go play. What's not to love about reasoning like that?

This same situation actually introduces the other concept I mentioned under supply and demand: investment versus consumption. Based on the piles of research I've waded through over the past few years, working an extra five hours a week wears down our bodies and our brains a fair bit. It increases stress levels and passes up opportunities for other things, like exercise or a creative hobby. If we spend our time today at the office, we get a little more money, but we've given up time now as well as time later. The reason we've used up time later is that we've used up our bodies a little sooner. In other words, our first option is consumption, where time from our "time account" has been spent; it's gone. The second option is more like an investment; we used this time to make even more time later.

Here's how those elements apply when it comes to something like a new car. Let's say, for argument's sake, that a person has forty years left to live. This will depend on whether he's learned his lesson about that third piece of pie, of course. If not, he may only have thirty-eight years left. Now, depending on his salary, if he buys a $40,000 car, then he's just spent most of a year. He is now down to thirty-nine years remaining. Maybe he makes a lot more than that in a year. Well, guess what, he already spent the extra time working last year to get that raise or promotion or position, so it's still a year gone. The scarcity of years is getting worse.

Instead, let's say he buys a $20,000 car and switches to a job with a lower salary but less overtime. Now he's only spent half of a year for the car expense and he will probably add half of a year to the end of his life because his stress level has gone down. This kind of reasoning has kept my income at the rusting, 1990 Geo Prizm level, instead of at the sleek, 2007 BMW level. The Sirens tell me I would look really good in a BMW too, but don't let my wife know.

A fancy car would not give me back more money than I spent on it. Above a basic threshold, the extra money spent on a car or the extra time spent at a job will give me smaller and smaller benefits. In contrast, the time I spend with my family does give me back extra time. The time I spend on my health does too.

To kind of bring into focus just how thoroughly capitalistic this whole line of thinking really is, imagine a bank account where the money disappears bit by bit every day whether you spend it or not. You can spend it on junk, you can invest it, or you can buy equipment that will help you earn additional money. Since economic, profit-driven, capitalist thinking says we should optimize value, we should be investing it or buying capital assets with it.

Now, let's combine that odd little bank account with a wondrous market opportunity. If you knew that next year there would only be forty diamonds left in the world, their price would go through the roof. That means every aspect of economic, capitalist rationality would impel you to buy diamonds at their relatively low price today—while you can.

By spending your time—from the declining bank account—on something other than just making more money, or getting more "stuff," which translates into the same thing, you are investing in an asset that is becoming more and more scarce every year. That's the very essence of a good, profit-maximizing investment. We don't need to switch to some different way of thinking; we just need to do a better job of following through on the type of thinking that's already built into our modern way of life.

The keystone in the whole process, though, is to realize that spending extra time, using up years of life, can get us more money (as with the example of going into the office on a Saturday afternoon). But later on, spending extra money cannot really get us more time, more years of life. In fact, a violation of that principle lies at the heart of the entire myth of retirement. We are not saving up for free time later by working extra now. We are cashing in retirement years of our life so we can work extra now. This kind of process is known in mathematics as a trapdoor function. It only goes one way, and once we go through, we can't come back.

When I am tempted to spend that same beautiful Saturday afternoon shopping for a new car, all of these elements of my business education come to the rescue. I can replace the car later if I neglect it a little now. (The

rust is not yet making the car go slower, so it's not cost-
ing me any time to have a little rust.) On the other hand,
I cannot really replace my body or my mind if I neglect
them. Oh, I could keep my out-dated, clunker of a body
running, but that's not really as good. In the same way, I
can't replace a perfect day making sand castles at the
beach with my daughter. My wife and I can't go back
later and spend a quiet weekend in the woods to celebrate
our fifteenth anniversary. Once those moments in time
are gone, they're gone for all time.

Unlike the story of the genie in the lamp, my story is
that we can effectively use one of our wishes to get more
wishes, or, in our case, use our time to get more time for
the satisfaction of enough. I'd love to stay and chat a little longer, but my daughter just came in and told me
there's a good kite wind blowing in from the northwest.

SIMPLICITY IN THE CITY

•

by Emily Houston

A<small>S A TWENTY-FOUR YEAR-OLD THIS YEAR, IT WAS VERY</small>
hard for me at first to think of a reason why I feel satisfied. The world around me moves at such a fast pace and
demands that everything happen in an instant. It's easy
to get lost in wanting more. Spending four hundred dollars on a pair of shoes, going out to dinner at expensive
restaurants, and having the world at the touch of a button on a phone the size of a palm . . . nothing is basic
anymore. It's so hard to feel fulfilled in a world that
teaches you to always want more.

However, I didn't always find myself living in a world
such as this. I grew up simply. My father was a Southern
Baptist minister in Georgia and my mother was a house-
wife. We lived twenty minutes away from any civiliza-
tion, and one of the most exciting events for me each
week was the tradition my father started when I began
school. Each Friday, he would pick me up from school
and let me pick out anything at the gas station that I
wanted. Meanwhile, my mom taught me respect for my
elders and the prayers that I still pray to this day.

Besides the gas station, all we had in our small town
was a post office, a general store, and several different
churches. There were only two other children my age, a

boy and a girl. We had the run of the town and got into trouble at every turn. It wasn't always easy living in a small town with nothing to do, but I believe that my creative imagination was formed in the Deep South.

When my father first told me years ago that we were going to move to upstate New York, I was both ecstatic and scared. On the one hand, at first I was excited to find myself in a new place that had a mall within a mile, and to find myself meeting new people with different accents, and living in a place where there was snow six months out of the year. But on the other hand, it was extremely hard to leave most of the people in my family with whom I was so close and to leave the simplicity of a small town behind. I was moving away from almost everyone I loved and everything I knew. However difficult, I embraced it as a new experience. I met friends then that I have to this day and I found out that I could survive in a place far different than what I was used to. I also found myself closer to my dream of living in New York City.

Six years ago a high school exchange program allowed me to visit one of the most exciting and creative cities in the world for two full weeks. I knew I had fallen in love the minute I stepped off the plane and got my first view of that famous New York City skyline. There would be no getting around it, I had to live there someday.

My parents always taught me the importance of education. Even though I thought I was ready when I moved out at eighteen, I knew that I needed to take small steps to prepare for the real world. So I threw myself into doing well in my college studies and making my parents proud. I was involved in the theater department at my school and many different organizations within the community. I made the dean's list every year. I worked hard, and even though I had to sacrifice some of the things I wanted, I knew the next step after college was not a move home. I moved to Brooklyn.

There are several things they don't teach you in college. I never learned the importance of a budget or that my GPA doesn't really mean a lot when I'm at a job interview. It's all about networking and who you know. Your degree is a nice piece of paper that doesn't hold a lot of water during interviews. The guidance counselors don't tell you that most people don't seem to read your resume; they judge a book by its cover letter, and appearance is everything. You may have a lot of talent, but if you don't have drive, you probably won't realize your goals. These were not the easiest thoughts to grasp so young, but they are important to know at the end of the day in order to handle the responsibility.

The first few months after my move to Brooklyn were all about adjusting—adjusting to these newfound realizations while trying to maintain a balance in my life that I have always made time for. I also found myself adjusting to living in a place that is completely different from any other place I have ever been. I had grown up living a very sheltered life, one that never included homeless people, public transportation, or fear in general. I now live in a place where I understand that if I don't work, I don't eat. If I don't make money, I won't make rent. These are the stresses I live with on a daily basis, just like everyone else around me. I find solace in this common ground among strangers who could at some point become friends.

While adjusting to my new life, I found that one of the hardest things I have had to learn is when to say no. I realize that I can't do everything I want and there's always going to be something I am missing out on, such as a show, a concert, a brunch with my boyfriend when I really want to stay in. I must prioritize and make sure that I'm doing what is important to me and what is fostering my creativity.

In order to live here in Brooklyn, I'm not able to do exactly what I want with each day. I think that this is a problem many Americans face today; we can't necessarily make our passion our job. In order to survive, we sometimes find ourselves in a job that barely uses our degree just so we can do those extra little things that mean so much: our hobbies, our down time, our family bonds— this is what makes it all worthwhile. At the end of a long day, my time is my own; it belongs to no one else. I now realize that this knowledge allows me that feeling of satisfaction I've been looking for.

I have a wonderful life outside of those mundane eight hours. My job is something I do for now. I don't let it define my happiness or peace with the world around me. I do struggle at times to keep a strong line drawn between what stays at work and what I drag home with me. If a supervisor yelled or if a coworker made a nasty comment, I find myself internalizing this, bringing my mood home sometimes.

It has always been very important to me to make sure that I do my best and show my best. A motto that my dad still loves to say and that I live by is "Remember you're a Houston." I am both indebted and grateful.

I have taken my simple upbringing and tried my best to incorporate it into my life. I have always made sure to take time for myself when I feel I'm becoming overwhelmed. I have discovered new ways to get over my stress, like taking a walk or treating myself to that extra bowl of ice cream. I don't deny myself the things that make me happy, I just make sure that I don't let them control me.

Often I find myself asking the questions, What am I doing with my life? Am I wasting precious time? After all, it's gone in an instant. But then I remember the beauty of simplicity that surrounds me every day. Taking a walk in the park on a warm spring day just when the cold weather has broken. Getting off the subway in Times Square every morning and seeing the Chrysler Building right in front of me.

I get the chance to attend some of the greatest shows on Broadway because of the little extra money I'm making. I love going to movies so I can get a huge tub of popcorn buttered in the middle. I am loved by my friends, by my boyfriend, and I have a very supportive and spiritual family. These are the things that get me through the day, that get me through the complications of this life.

I carry the knowledge with me that each day is a blessing and the people I meet along the way make it that much sweeter.

THE BRASS RING

•

by Steven Fisher

A FEW YEARS BACK I WAS WORKING AS A TECHNICAL consultant and life was perfect. I was at a high point in my life. I was paid excellent money to travel around the country and direct high-value projects concerning corporate mergers. I had a great wife, three wonderful kids, a mid-six-figure income, an airplane that I was paid to fly, a big house, and a $1,000 watch that I wore proudly and prominently everywhere I went. I hadn't managed to save much, but what was the use when we had so much cash flow coming in every two weeks.

Then the great consulting job I held threatened to come to an end as the company was restructuring and eliminating all consulting positions. This actually happened a few times during my tenure, since a merger causes a company to rethink operational procedures. I could have taken on a permanent position at a lower salary, which I didn't want to do, or I could have tried to gain a consulting assignment in a different area of the corporation, which was a decreasing possibility with each passing day.

There also came a point when the puzzle pieces didn't quite seem to be fitting into place. I was missing out on my children's growth, as I was on the road so much, and

I felt that life had so much more to offer. Sure we'd jump in the airplane and shoot down to Florida on a free weekend, but I was missing the daily activities like the kids' basketball games and school programs, the important stuff. I could tell that my kids were missing me too. My wife and I had a serious meeting, prayed, and decided that it might be time for a career change.

Since I was very experienced in the business arena and had obviously shown that I knew how to make money, I naively felt that the world of business was fully open for my exploration. We talked about options and about our wishes, and we finally decided that I would jump into the mergers and acquisitions field. I had the fundraising experience, knew how to value a business, and surely could sell anything. It was perfect!

We had enough money in the bank to carry us for six months at our customary spending level, and we felt that there would be little to no startup cost for this new venture. As often happens in situations like this, hindsight is 20/20. There were many startup issues that we hadn't seen, and many pieces had to be put in place to get the business on the right track. There were two main issues that we had overlooked. Number one was the sales cycle, which is the amount of time it takes to set up and close a deal (six months or more in mergers and acquisitions) and number two was the reputation factor, which is built by advertising, networking, and having a successful track record.

Although I was well known in the technical arena, I had no established reputation in mergers and acquisitions. I got many sideways looks when I talked to business owners about selling their businesses. They would ask how many businesses I had sold and I had to say that I was involved in the sales of several businesses, but hadn't directly sold any. This made it hard to gain any clients, let alone sell any businesses.

As it turns out, my eyes and my head were bigger than my abilities and, as you can guess, the money trickled away faster than we had planned. We had our standard of living to maintain, an awesome amount of bills to pay each month, and our airplane to pay for and maintain, since it was no longer being subsidized. It was an expensive enjoyment that we continued to use, and we soon came to a point where we needed some income if we were to survive.

As we prayed and pondered this, I was reminded that we had assets that had been purchased during our high times, and we could look at selling those to help maintain our lifestyle or at least keep up with the bills. We felt it was just a short-term fix, as surely the mergers and acquisitions field would provide for us in the near future.

Eventually, we ended up selling our apartment complex and, painfully for me, we were obliged to sell our airplane as well. If you knew the passion I have for aviation and knew how difficult it was for me to sell it, you would begin to understand the seriousness of the situation we were diving into. Though I felt I was walking with God throughout, I was still headstrong and was sure that I could make mergers and acquisitions work for us. However, I did begin to realize that you can have your cake and eat it too—unless the cake is too expensive to afford.

After a time, things got worse. Life was not perfect anymore. We had taken on so much debt, which is easy to do, and had little income from the business, so we were now struggling to pay the bills. We were also having a hard time putting food on the table. Have you ever been to the grocery store and the person in front of you puts something back because they don't have enough money to buy everything in the cart? Well, that person was me, and oftentimes it was milk or eggs I was putting back. (If I see that situation today, I pull out some dollar bills and quietly lay them on the counter to pay for what they cannot.)

As a father of three, I can tell you that this was a heartbreaker. It literally drove me to my knees in prayer. Many times during this phase of our journey, either someone we knew, or someone we did not know, would bring us food to eat. A miracle? You bet! Where did the people hear that we were in need of food and how did they know where we lived? We had shared the situation we were in with only a select few. We were on a path with God and this journey would take us to the depths of the valley, only to restore us again with a changed perspective.

Please understand that this entire situation was very difficult for me. I was a person who held myself in high esteem. When I needed housework done, I hired it out. When I felt I needed something or wanted a new toy, I simply paid for it. Whether we bought things on cash or credit, it didn't matter. I would even hesitate to go into the Kmart store for fear I would be seen by someone I knew. I was conceited and snobbish, and I had the money and debt to prove it. I held the "brass ring."

We came to a realization point that I hope we almost all come to sooner or later in life, even if others' situations are not as drastic as ours. We take a good, hard look at what we're doing and for what purpose. It is a point that has a tendency to redefine who we are and also redefine our wants and needs.

We did a lot of adjusting. Since we were so low on cash and income, we had to adjust our way of thinking. We dropped our wants, realigned our goals to serving God, surviving, and paying bills. We also adjusted our expectations.

We felt as if we were at the bottom, and decided that mergers and acquisitions was not where we were supposed to be. I attempted to step back into the technical arena to earn a living but this was not easy, as I had been out of the game for a time and lost momentum. Finally, I was able to get a job with a local franchise as a technician, and it brought in a little money but not enough. We had to get some additional cash coming in, so I took a second job as a newspaper delivery person.

Having to hold two jobs that didn't pay very well was a learning experience for me, as I had always held jobs that I viewed as dignified. I'm not saying that a job as a technician or a newspaper delivery person is not dignified, but at that point in time this was my view. Ironically, I had directed many technicians in my former career, and now I was one.

I was working hard and bringing in money. Thankfully, I could now feed my kids and pay my bills, and after a short time the mighty attitude about myself was gracefully changed. The situation was looking better, we were starting to feel better, and praises flowed heavenward. There was a new sense of pride and accomplishment in the work I did that was never present before. I was working two jobs, waking at 2:30 a.m. and working until 7:00 p.m., with some flexibility, and I liked it! Wow!

On my previous job I had always felt that I was paid well for the consulting work I did. I sat in meetings, directed people, made difficult decisions, and got things done—but I never broke a sweat. I had paid a hefty price for that job in other ways, though. I had no free time and was not able to choose when to be with my family, and there was a lot of stress as well. On reflection, I can see that while I was in that career I had no real sense of accomplishment in the work that I did, and it seemed empty and lacking in joy. Now, I am earning a real, hard-working living!

It makes one think, though. Would I rather have a high-paying job with lots of money even if the job controls me, or a job that provides enough for me to live on but gives me time to enjoy life and also gives me a sense of accomplishment that makes me happy?

Is this the balancing point? It was for me. I found that I am happier when I'm working hard and earning a living for it, serving God and praying. I now have time that I can spend with my family and have a great sense of accomplishment every day.

We are very conservative with our money at this point and resist the urge to buy frivolous stuff. We shop at a discount grocery store and always pay in cash and, yes, we shop at Kmart too. We are now starting to climb out of debt and live more comfortably, which I would tend to say is more Spartan than the average American lifestyle, since we have really adjusted what we need to live on in order to be satisfied. Life is good.

So I recommend that people evaluate their lives. Let's step back and look at our situations. Let's look at what our wants, needs, and goals are. Do we really need all the stuff we have? How many cars are enough, and how big does our house have to be? Are we living beyond our means? You can learn from my experience and adjust before there is a crisis. How much is enough?

About the Authors

•

STEPHANIE BARTON is a freelance writer and editor. She lives in Hawaii with her husband and a small, fat dog.

MICHAEL BECK, a retired schoolteacher, lives in Glendale in the Los Angeles area, not ten miles from where he was born. He enjoys travel, especially in nature, and has never met a national or state park, monument, forest, or wildlife preserve that he didn't love. He relishes foreign languages, with a soft spot for English in which he writes for fun; he reads history and popular science for pleasure and devours science fiction. He joins friends for good conversations over meals (healthy food these days) and heads a local Sierra Club program, Dine for Your Health and Your Planet's Health.

TAMSEN BUTLER is a freelance writer and editor. Although she now resides in the Midwest with her husband, Scott, and her children, Monet and Abram, she has been fortunate to live all over the world.

FRED ECKS worked as a corporate software engineer for many years before happening upon the program in the book *Your Money or Your Life* by Joe Dominguez and Vicki Robin. He diligently applied the steps in his own life, paying off his debt and eventually becoming financially independent when he was thirty-five years old. Since then, he has enjoyed a life blending a variety of volunteer work and personal enrichment. Fred can usually be found doing something outside. He's an avid ultramarathon runner, backpacker, and sailor. He lives with his sweetie and a curmudgeon cat on a small boat on the San Francisco Bay.

STEVEN FISHER is married to an Angel, is a father of three, and lives happily in the north central United States. He has successfully started over ten companies and currently owns a computer service franchise in which he still works as a technician. He now has ample time for God, friends, and family.

TEENA HAMMOND GOMEZ is a journalist who has been on staff at many top magazines, including being a correspondent for the Los Angeles bureau of *People* magazine, West Coast retail editor for *Women's Wear Daily*, writer of features and fashion for *W* magazine, and senior writer for *In Touch Weekly*. She is currently a freelance writer, living in Shelbyville, Kentucky, and writing for various national and local publications, both print and online. In 2006 she moved back to her native state of Kentucky after living in Arizona and California for seventeen years. She lives with her husband, Joe, and their three golden retrievers, Clifford, Neil, and Moses, as well as their cat, Streak.

DEREK DONALD HAMBRICK, father to Gabriel and husband to Carmen, tries to keep his priorities straight. Five years after realizing he wanted to write for a living, Derek completed his bachelor of arts in communication and rhetoric studies at Oglethorpe University, ten years to the day after earning his first degree, also from Oglethorpe. Between degrees, he married his sweetie pie and welcomed their son to a world that the couple is intent on improving, one family (and one publication) at a time. Derek works with youth across the United States and Canada through Sukyo Mahikari, a nonprofit, community service organization. The Hambricks reside (for now) in Decatur, Georgia, but yearn for the Pacific Northwest.

KATHERINE HAUSWIRTH is a writer (technical by day, creative by stolen moments) who lives near the Connecticut shoreline. Her blog, *Inching Toward Simplicity: Pragmatics and Prose* (http://inchingsimplicity.blogspot.com), includes both real-life tips and philosophical musings on the effort to simplify. She has been published in *The Writer, The Writer's Handbook 2003, Pregnancy, Pilgrimage, Snowy Egret, Funds for Writers, Writers Weekly,* and many other print and online publications. Her first book, *Things My Mother Told Me: Reflections on Parenthood,* is available on Amazon.com.

BETH HERNDON is a twenty-something southerner who works as a neurology nurse at a large hospital in Tennessee. She loves helping people every day, as well as the challenges that come with the health care field. She also loves the outdoors and takes part in adventures anytime she gets the chance. Reading e.e. cummings, C. S. Lewis, and the newspaper are other passions. Most of all, she enjoys all things natural.

BOB HINSCHLÄGER enjoys the simple pleasures of life in rural Ohio where, as a boy, he scoured fields for Indian artifacts and woods for natural wonders. Today Bob, an engineer with a Fortune 500 company, is blessed to share a Christian home with his wife, Becky, and their family, where he enthusiastically pursues freelance writing, designing and building wood furniture, vegetable gardening, and discovering history. He recently completed the chronicle of his father's World War II navy experiences.

CAROL HOLST is founder of Postconsumers, an educational company helping to move our society beyond addictive consumerism.. She is an advisory board member of the *Simple Living with Wanda Urbanska* national public television series and a liaison member of the Sierra Club Sustainable Consumption Committee. Based in the Los Angeles area, Carol especially enjoys hiking, modeling, and chocolate-covered nuts. She adores her two grown daughters in the ultrafast lane, both born on her birthday five years apart. Someday she hopes to Get Satisfied.

EMILY HOUSTON has been telling her stories ever since she can remember. She lives in Brooklyn, New York, freelance writing and working an eight-hour day. This is her first published essay, and she couldn't be happier that it's for a concept as true as this—live simply.

LIZ MILNER is a native of Washington, D.C., and a reforming clutter queen. When she is not sorting through her stuff, she works as a freelance writer, with articles published in the *Washington Post, Renaissance Magazine, Old Time Herald Magazine, Green Man Review,* and the *Alexandria Gazette.* She is a founder of the Reston Community Center's Writers Group in Reston, Virginia. Her hobbies include folk music, running, and cooking. After twenty years in northern

Virginia, she just moved to the Philadelphia, Pennsylvania area where she is feverishly unpacking.

JON MYHRE practiced architecture and landscape architecture in Los Angeles and Pasadena for over forty years before retiring to Ojai, California, after the passing of his wife. Among his hundreds of projects are city and county parks, college campuses, airports, historical preservations, and residential work of every description. Since moving to Ojai, he has turned his major creative efforts to writing. His short stories, columns, and poetry have been published in major newspapers; he is currently working on his first novel. He travels extensively and spends quality time with his two daughters and two grandchildren.

J. EVA NAGEL is enjoying the journey in upstate New York. She is a psychotherapist in private practice, consultant, writer, and storyteller. She has been following in the footsteps of her ancestors, working for young people and social justice most of her life. In 1983 she founded the Waldorf School of Saratoga Springs and in 1986 cofounded Side By Side, a youth leadership service program. Her written creations have appeared in magazines and journals, and on public radio. Her gardens and murals beckon. Most important, she is famous as the wife of one, the mother of four, and the head-over-heels proud grandmother of two.

TODRA PAYNE writes articles and produces photo shoots for lifestyle and inspirational magazines. She has also coauthored two career guides, *Fabjob Guide to Become a Makeup Artist* and *Fabjob Guide to Become a Spa Owner.* Her first novel, *Chasing*

Jesus through Greenwich Village, is complete and seeking a publishing home. It's a funny tale about a spunky young woman's search for self while juggling her on-again, off-again love life and her quirky, demanding job as a fashion stylist for the rich and famous in New York City. Todra lives in Pennsylvania, but escapes to New York often.

RUTH PITTARD is a native North Carolinian, baby boomer, and trained teacher who learned to live simply from watching her grandmother and mother, and from reading visionary writers. After thirty years in higher education, Ruth now delivers life coaching, creates transformational menopause workshops, and teaches people of all ages and stages how to live lightly on the earth. She is also a trained facilitator for the Awakening the Dreamer symposium created by the Pachamama Alliance (www.pachamama.org). Mother of two, grandmother to three, and family for many, Ruth practices living an intentionally peaceful, holistic existence. She is at home wherever life sends her.

ERIK RICHARDSON lives in Milwaukee, Wisconsin, with his wife, his daughter, and a really worn-out car. When he isn't outside playing, or writing about how he should be outside playing, he works as an independent management consultant helping small business owners spend less time and make more money.

BRIAN SIMKINS lives in Chicago, Illinois, with his wife, Jamie. They spend as much of their free time as possible enjoying the outdoors and traveling to see friends and family.

ANDREW VIETZE is a park ranger and Maine-based free-lance writer. The former managing editor of *Down East: The Magazine of Maine*, he's written for a wide array of publications, from *Time Out New York* to *Offshore* to *AMC Outdoors* to *Hooked on the Outdoors* (among many others). He's the author of a guidebook to the coast of Maine, and he's working on a nonfiction book about a famous Maine guide who played a huge role in the making of Teddy Roosevelt. He writes a blog about life as a park ranger (www.downeast.com) and spends as much time as he can adventuring with his wife, Lisa, and son, Gus.

GALEN WARDEN was raised on a slim budget by a single mother who was active in the civil rights movement of the 1960s. She also spent vacations, complete with yacht clubs and sailing trips, with her father in the Connecticut suburbs. This dual citizenship, of privilege and humble means, provided Galen with a rare opportunity to develop an informed opinion of the world and her place in it. Always eager to travel, always ready to help others, this poet and writer is also an artist and designer—seeking to make her loving mark on the world, beyond providing it with her six wonderful children.

PETER C. WHYBROW, M.D. is director of the Semel Institute for Neuroscience and Human Behavior at the University of California in Los Angeles. His most recent book, *American Mania: When More Is Not Enough*, is a provocative neurobiological analysis of the instinctual and social behaviors that balance a market economy. *American Mania* explains how

America's affluent and reward-driven migrant culture is in danger of losing that balance, making itself sick in body and mind as it pushes the physiological limits of our evolutionary inheritance.

Simple Living Resources

•

The following list of simple living resources was prepared by The Simple Living Network (www.simpleliving.net). The Simple Living Network is a central location on the Internet where you will find a wide variety of these types of resources, as well as tools, examples, and contacts for conscious, simple, healthy, and restorative living.

Alvord, Katie. Divorce Your Car! Ending the Love Affair with the Automobile. Gabriola Island, Canada: New Society Publishers, 2000.

Andrews, Cecile. The Circle of Simplicity: Return to the Good Life. New York: HarperPerennial, 1997.

————. Slow Is Beautiful: New Visions of Community, Leisure and Joie de Vivre. Gabriola Island, Canada: New Society Publishers, 2006.

Aslett, Don. Clutter's Last Stand: It's Time to De-Junk Your Life, 2nd ed. Avon, MA: Adams Media, 2005.

Bee-Gates, Donna. I Want It Now: Navigating Childhood in a Materialistic World. New York: Palgrave Macmillan, 2006.

Berthold-Bond, Annie. Better Basics for the Home: Simple Solutions for Less Toxic Living. New York: Three Rivers Press, 1999.

————. Clean & Green: The Complete Guide to Nontoxic and Environmentally Safe Housekeeping, 2nd ed. Woodstock, NY: Ceres Press, 1994.

Blix, Jacqueline and David Heitmiller. Getting a Life: Strategies for Simple Living Based on the Revolutionary Program for Financial Freedom, Your Money or Your Life. New York: Penguin, 1997.

Brill, Hal et al. Investing with Your Values: Making Money and Making a Difference. Rev/ ed., Gabriola Island, Canada: New Society Publishers, 2000.

Brower, Michael and Warren Leon. The Consumer's Guide to Effective Environmental Choices: Practical Advice from the Union of Concerned Scientists. New York: Three Rivers Press, 1999.

Callenbach, Ernest. Living Cheaply with Style: Live Better and Spend Less. Berkeley: Ronin Publishing, 2000.

Camejo, Peter. The SRI Advantage: Why Socially Responsible Investing Has Outperformed Financially. Gabriola Island, Canada: New Society Publishers, 2002.

Campbell, Jeff. Speed Cleaning. New York: Dell Publishing, 1997.

Campbell, Jeff and Clean Team Staff. Clutter Control: Putting Your Home on a Diet. New York: Dell Publishing Company, 1992.

Chiars, Dan and Dave Wann. Superbia! 31 Ways to Create Sustainable Neighborhoods. Gabriola Island, Canada: New Society Publishers, 2003.

Cox, Connie and Chris Evatt. 30 Days to a Simpler Life. New York: Plume Books, 1998.

Dacyczyn, Amy. The Complete Tightwad Gazette: Promoting Thrift as a Viable Alternative Lifestyle. New York: Villard Books, 1998.

de Graaf, John, ed. Take Back Your Time: Fighting Overwork and Time Poverty in America. San Francisco: Berrett-Koehler Publishers, 2003.

de Graaf, John et al. Affluenza: The All-Consuming Epidemic. San Francisco: Berrett-Koehler Publishers, 2005.

de Graaf, John, producer. Affluenza (DVD). Oley, PA: Bullfrog Films, 1997.

————— . Escape from Affluenza: Living Better on Less (DVD). Oley, PA: Bullfrog Films, 1998.

Doherty, William J. et al. Putting Family First: Successful Strategies for Reclaiming Family Life in a Hurry-Up World. New York: Owl Books, 2002.

Dominguez, Joe. Transforming Your Relationship with Money: The Nine-Step Program for Achieving Financial Integrity, Intelligence, and Independence (CD/Workbook Course). Boulder: Sounds True, 2005.

Dominguez, Joe and Vicki Robin. Your Money or Your Life: Transforming Your Relationship with Money and Achieving Financial Independence. New York: Penguin, 1992.

Domini, Amy. Socially Responsible Investing: Making a Difference and Making Money. Chicago: Dearborn Trade, 2001.

Dungan, Nathan. Prodigal Sons & Material Girls: How Not to Be Your Child's ATM. Hoboken: John Wiley & Sons, 2003.

Durning, Alan. How Much Is Enough? The Consumer Society and the Future of the Earth. New York: W.W. Norton & Company, 1992.

Elgin, Duane. Voluntary Simplicity: Toward a Way of Life

That Is Outwardly Simple, Inwardly Rich. New York: Harper, 1993.

————. Promise Ahead: A Vision of Hope and Action for Humanity's Future. New York: Quill, 2001.

Elkin, Bruce. Simplicity & Success: Creating the Life You Long For. Victoria, Canada: Trafford Publishing, 2003.

Emery, Carla. The Encyclopedia of Country Living. Seattle: Sasquatch Books, 1994.

Everett, Melissa. Making a Living While Making a Difference: The Expanded Guide to Creating Careers with a Conscience. Gabriola Island, Canada: New Society Publishers, 1999.

Fogler, Michael. Un-Jobbing: The Adult Liberation Handbook. Lexington, KY: Free Choice Press, 2003.

Foster, Richard J. Freedom of Simplicity: Finding Harmony in a Complex World. New York: HarperPaperbacks, 1981.

Harnden, Philip, ed. Journeys of Simplicity: Traveling Light with Thomas Merton, Basho, Edward Abbey, Annie Dillard & Others. Woodstock, VT: Skylight Paths Publishing, 2007.

Honore, Carl. In Praise of Slowness: How a Worldwide Movement Is Challenging the Cult of Speed. New York: HarperCollins, 2004.

Josefine, Claire. The Spiritual Art of Being Organized. Eureka, CA: Winter's Daughter Press, 2004.

————. The 12 Basic Principles of Being Organized: 60 Tips Toward a Serene Life. Eureka, CA: Winter's Daughter Press, 2003.

Kasser, Tim. The High Price of Materialism. Cambridge: The MIT Press, 2003.

Kozin, Michelle. Organic Weddings: Balancing Ecology,

Style and Tradition. Gabriola Island, Canada: New Society Publishers, 2003.

Kruse, Jym, ed. Songs & Stories of Simple Living. Sioux City: Alternatives for Simple Living, 1997.

Lehmkuhl, Dorothy and Dolores Cotter Lamping. Organizing for the Creative Person: Right-Brain Styles for Conquering Clutter, Mastering Time, and Reaching Your Goals. New York: Three Rivers Press, 1993.

Levering, Frank and Wanda Urbanska. Simple Living: One Couple's Search for a Better Life. Winston-Salem: John F. Blair, 2003.

Levine, Judith. Not Buying It: My Year Without Shopping. New York: Free Press, 2006.

Longacre, Doris Janzen. Living More with Less. Scottdale, PA: Herald Press, 1980.

——. More-With-Less Cookbook, 2nd ed. Scottdale, PA: Herald Press, 2000.

Luhrs, Janet. The Simple Living Guide: A Sourcebook for Less Stressful, More Joyful Living. New York: Broadway Books, 1997.

McBay, Aric. Peak Oil Survival: Preparation for Life After Gridcrash. Guilford, CT: The Lyons Press, 2006.

McCoy, Jonni. Miserly Moms: Living on One Income in a Two Income Economy, 3rd ed. Bloomington, MN: Bethany House Publishers, 2001.

Merkel, Jim. Radical Simplicity: Small Footprints on a Finite Planet. Gabriola Island, Canada: New Society Publishers, 2003.

——. RADICALLY simple (DVD). Oley, PA: Bullfrog Films, 2005.

Mundis, Jerrold. How to Get Out of Debt, Stay Out of

Debt, & Live Prosperously. New York: Bantam Books, 1988.

Nattrass, Brian and Mary Altomare. The Natural Step for Business: Wealth, Ecology and the Evolutionary Corporation. Gabriola Island, Canada: New Society Publishers, 1999.

Nearing, Scott and Helen Nearing. The Good Life: Helen and Scott Nearing's Sixty Years of Self-Sufficient Living. New York: Schocken Books, 1989.

Petrini, Carlo et al. Slow Food: Collected Thoughts on Taste, Tradition, and Honest Pleasures of Food. White River Junction, VT: Chelsea Green Company, 2001.

Pierce, Linda Breen. Choosing Simplicity: Real People Finding Peace and Fulfillment in a Complex World. Carmel: Gallagher Press, 2000.

———Simplicity Lessons: A 12-Step Guide to Living Simply. Carmel: Gallagher Press, 2003.

Robert, Karl-Henrik. The Natural Step Story: Seeding a Quiet Revolution. Gabriola Island, Canada: New Society Publishers, 2002.

Robinson, Jo and Jean Coppock Staeheli. Unplug the Christmas Machine: A Complete Guide to Putting Love and Joy Back into the Season. New York: Quill, 1991.

Ryan, John C. and Alan Thein Durning. Stuff: The Secret Lives of Everyday Things. Seattle: Northwest Environment Watch, 1997.

Salomon, Shay. Little House on a Small Planet: Simple Homes, Cozy Retreats, and Energy Efficient Possibilities. Guilford, CT: The Lyons Press, 2006.

Sandbeck, Ellen. Organic Housekeeping. New York: Scribner, 2006.

Schor, Juliet B. Born to Buy: The Commercialized Child and the New Consumer Culture. New York: Scribner, 2004.

———. The Overspent American: Why We Want What We Don't Need. New York: Harper Perennial, 1999.

———. The Overworked American: The Unexpected Decline of Leisure. New York: Basic Books, 1993.

Schumacher, E. F. Small Is Beautiful: Economics as if People Mattered. Point Roberts, WA: Hartley & Marks Publishers, 1973.

Schut, Michael et al. Simpler Living, Compassionate Life. New York: Living the Good News, 1999.

Segal, Jerome M. Graceful Simplicity: The Philosophy and Politics of the Alternative American Dream. Reprint, Berkeley: University of California Press, 2002.

Sherlock, Marie. Living Simply with Children: A Voluntary Simplicity Guide for Moms, Dads, and Kids Who Want to Reclaim the Bliss of Childhood and the Joy of Parenting. New York: Three Rivers Press, 2003.

Silver, Don. High School Money Book. Los Angeles: Adams-Hall Publishing, 2006.

Silver, Susan. Organized to Be Your Best: Transforming How You Work. Los Angeles: Adams-Hall Publishing, 2006.

Smallin, Donna. Organizing Plain & Simple: A Ready Reference Guide with Hundreds of Solutions to Your Everyday Clutter Challenges. North Adams, MA: Storey Publishing, 2002.

———. Unclutter Your Home: 7 Simple Steps, 700 Tips & Ideas. North Adams, MA: Storey Publishing, 1999.

St. James, Elaine. Simplify Your Christmas: 100 Ways to Reduce the Stress and Recapture the Joy of the Holidays. Kansas City, MO: Andrews McMeel Publishing, 1998.

Storey, John and Martha Storey. Storey's Basic Country Skills: A Practical Guide to Self-Reliance. North Adams, MA: Storey Publishing, 1999.

Susanka, Sarah. The Not So Big Life: Making Room for What Really Matters. New York: Random House, 2007.

Taylor, Betsy. What Kids Really Want That Money Can't Buy: Tips for Parenting in a Commercial World. New York: Time Warner Book Group, 2003.

Taylor-Hough, Deborah. A Simple Choice: A Practical Guide for Saving Your Time, Money and Sanity. Belgium, WI: Champion Press, 2000.

Thoreau, Henry David. Walden. 1854. Reprint, Boston: Beacon Press, 2004.

Twigg, Nancy. Celebrate Simply: Your Guide to Simpler, More Meaningful Holidays and Special Occasions. Grand Rapids: Kregel Publications, 2006.

Urbanska, Wanda and Frank Levering. Nothing's Too Small to Make a Difference. Winston-Salem: John F. Blair, 2004.

———. Moving to a Small Town: A Guide for Moving from Urban to Rural America. New York: Fireside, 1996.

———. Simple Living with Wanda Urbanska (Seasons 1–3 DVD). Mount Airy, NC: The Simple Living Company, 2004–2007.

Wackernagel, Mathis. The Ecological Footprint: Accounting for a Small Planet (DVD). Oley, PA: Bullfrog Films, 2004.

Wackernagel, Mathis and William Rees. Our Ecological Footprint: Reducing Human Impact on the Earth. Gabriola Island, Canada: New Society Publishers, 1996.

White, John L. My Job Sucks & I Can't Take It Anymore! Help! The Real-Life Survival Guide. Wesley Chapel, FL: Everlove and Bohannon Publishing, 2007.

White, John L. I'm In Debt, Over 40, with No Retirement Savings, HELP! How to Get Out of Debt and Start Saving for Retirement Now. Wesley Chapel, FL: Everlove and Bohannon Publishing, 2004.

Whitmire, Catherine. Plain Living: A Quaker Path to Simplicity, Notre Dame: Sorin Books, 2001.

Whybrow, Peter C. American Mania: When More Is Not Enough. New York: W.W. Norton & Company, 2005.

Willand, Lois Carlson. The Use-It-Up Cookbook: A Guide for Minimizing Food Waste. Minneapolis: Practical Cookbooks, 1979.

Wilson, Alex et al. Consumer Guide to Home Energy Savings. Washington, DC: American Council for an Energy-Efficient Economy, 2003.

Zelinski, Ernie J. The Joy of Not Working: A Book for the Retired, Unemployed, and Overworked. Berkeley: Ten Speed Press, 2003.